A
LONE STAR
COWBOY

A LONE STAR COWBOY

by
Charles Angelo Siringo

New Foreword
by
Marc Simmons

SOUTHWEST HERITAGE SERIES

SUNSTONE
PRESS

SANTA FE

❋ ❋ ❋

Susie and Bill Robertson are pleased
to share their appreciation
for their Texas heritage
by underwriting this historic book.

❋ ❋ ❋

New Material © 2006 by Sunstone Press. All Rights Reserved.

Sunstone books may be purchased for educational, business, or sales promotional use.
For information please write: Special Markets Department, Sunstone Press,
P.O. Box 2321, Santa Fe, New Mexico 87504-2321.

Library of Congress Cataloging-in-Publication Data:

Siringo, Charles A.,1855–1928.
A Lone Star cowboy / by Charles Angelo Siringo ; new foreword by Marc Simmons.
    p.cm. -- (Southwest heritage series)
Originally published: Santa Fe, N.M. : [s.n.], 1919.
ISBN: 0-86534-533-3 (alk. paper)
    1. Siringo, Charles A., 1855–1928. 2. Cowboys--West (U.S.)--Biography.
3. Cowboys--Texas--Biography. 4. Frontier and pioneer life--West (U.S.)
5. Frontier and pioneer life--Texas. 6. Peace officers--New Mexico--Biography.
7. Billy, the Kid. 8. West (U.S.)--Biography. 9. Texas--Biography.
10. Private investigators--United States--Biography. I. Title.

F596.S534 2006
976.4'06092--dc22
[B]
                                        2006044383

Published in

WWW.SUNSTONEPRESS.COM
SUNSTONE PRESS / POST OFFICE BOX 2321 / SANTA FE, NM 87504-2321 /USA
(505) 988-4418 / ORDERS ONLY (800) 243-5644 / FAX (505) 988-1025

The Southwest Heritage Series is dedicated
to Jody Ellis and Marcia Muth Miller,
the founders of Sunstone Press,
whose original purpose and vision continues
to inspire and motivate our publications.

CONTENTS

I

THE SOUTHWEST HERITAGE SERIES

The history of the United States is written in hundreds of regional histories and literary works. Those letters, essays, memoirs, biographies and even collections of fiction are often first-hand accounts by people who wanted to memorialize an event, a person or simply record for posterity the concerns and issues of the times. Many of these accounts have been lost, destroyed or overlooked. Some are in private or public collections but deemed to be in too fragile condition to permit handling by contemporary readers and researchers.

However, now with the application of twenty-first century technology, nineteenth and twentieth century material can be reprinted and made accessible to the general public. These early writings are the DNA of our history and culture and are essential to understanding the present in terms of the past.

The Southwest Heritage Series is a form of literary preservation. Heritage by definition implies legacy and these early works are our legacy from those who have gone before us. To properly present and preserve that legacy, no changes in style or contents have been made. The material reprinted stands on its own as it first appeared. The point of view is that of the author and the era in which he or she lived. We would not expect photographs of people from the past to be re-imaged with modern clothes, hair styles and backgrounds. We should not, therefore, expect their ideas and personal philosophies to reflect our modern concepts.

Remember, reading their words and sharing their thoughts is a passport back into understanding how the past was shaped and how it influenced today's world.

Our hope is that new access to these older books will provide readers with a challenging and exciting experience.

II

FOREWORD TO THIS EDITION
by
Marc Simmons

For a number of years prior to 1922, one of Santa Fe, New Mexico's most colorful and famous residents was Charles Angelo Siringo (1855-1928), popularly known as "the cowboy detective." A small, wiry man, he was friends with practically everyone in town, from the governor to the dog catcher.

In 1916 Governor William C. McDonald persuaded Siringo to accept a commission as a New Mexico Mounted Ranger for the state Cattle Sanitary Board. The only thing unusual about that was Charlie Siringo's age, a ripe 61. Undaunted, he saddled up and with a pack horse started for his headquarters at Carrizozo in Lincoln County.

His duty was to run down outlaws and stock thieves in southern New Mexico. Bill Owens, described as a fighting son-of-a-gun, became his partner. As Siringo reported later, "Poor Bill lasted only a short time."

The pair got into a gun fight with cattle thieves at Abo Pass east of Belen. Owens was shot through the lungs, but he emptied his pistol and killed two of the outlaws before he went down.

"During my two years as a ranger," Siringo said, "I made many arrests of cattle and horse thieves and had many close calls with death staring me in the face." Obviously, Governor McDonald had made a wise choice when he tapped this hard-riding, fast-shooting "senior citizen" for the dangerous ranger job.

Charlie Siringo's career in the West was as adventurous as it was long. Raised in Matagorda County, Texas, he took to life in the saddle before he was shaving.

As he put it, "When I was twelve years of age, in the spring of 1867, I became a full-fledged cowboy, wearing broad sombrero, high-heeled boots, Mexican spurs and the dignity of a full-grown man."

After trips up the Chisholm Trail, he landed a cowboy job in the Texas Panhandle, still a teenager. He fought prairie fires, had run-ins with rustlers and saw the last herds of buffalo roaming the Staked Plains.

The years drifted by and Charlie Siringo drifted with them. At age thirty he was tending store at Caldwell, Kansas and putting in nights writing up his previous experiences on the range.

When his book, *A Texas Cowboy*, appeared, its author achieved fame overnight. Eventually, it sold a million copies. *A Lone Star Cowboy*, published in 1919, contained many of the stories in his earlier book and the author says in his preface: "This volume is to take the place of *A Texas Cowboy*...." The latter portion of the book dealt with his life as a Kansas merchant, as a Pinkerton detective, and his term as a member of the New Mexico Mounted Rangers who concentrated on tracking down rustlers.

Meanwhile, soon after publishing his recollections, Siringo joined the renowned Pinkerton Detective Agency, whose branch offices covered the West. He remained with the firm for two decades, getting in and out of more scrapes than a modern TV sleuth.

The Pinkerton men first gained national attention just before the Civil War when they foiled a plot to assassinate Lincoln on the way to his inauguration. Later they made headlines in trying to break up Jesse James' gang, an effort that cost several detectives their lives.

Pinkertons were often hired as strike-breakers. They proved so successful that they earned the bitter hatred of organized unions. Siringo participated in one episode at Coeur d'Alene, Idaho.

There in 1892 occurred huge labor riots attended by the dynamiting of mines and the murder of managers. In trials that followed, Agent Siringo gave crucial testimony that led to the conviction of eighteen union leaders for these crimes. Soon afterward, the home office sent him in pursuit of Butch Cassidy's Wild Bunch.

After leaving the Pinkertons, Charlie Siringo returned to the Southwest and did a good bit of roaming before settling in Santa Fe.

Because of the name he'd made in publishing, he had access to many persons, on both sides of the law, who were on their way to winning a place in the history books. From them he got first hand information that he later incorporated in a new book called *Riata and Spurs*.

In that work, the writer had wanted to include some of his own daring adventures while serving with the Pinkertons. But the Agency threatened a lawsuit if he revealed any of their professional secrets. So the cowboy detective had to delete some of his best material.

Siringo in his later years lived in near poverty, making small amounts of money from his book writing and consulting on western films for Hollywood producers.

Charles Angelo Siringo fell victim to a heart attack on October 8, 1928 in Altadena, California. Humorist Will Rogers, who knew and respected him, sent a telegram upon learning of his passing. It read: "May flowers always grow over his grave."

III

FACSIMILE OF 1919 EDITION

A LONE STAR COWBOY

Being fifty years experience in the saddle as Cowboy, Detective and New Mexico Ranger, on every
cow trail in the wooly old west.   Also the doings
of some "bad" cowboys, such as "Billy the Kid",
Wess Harding and "Kid Curry".   ::   ::   ::   ::

By CHAS. A. SIRINGO

Author of "Fifteen Years on the Hurricane Deck
of a Spanish Pony" and "A Cowboy Detective".

SANTA FE, NEW MEXICO

1919

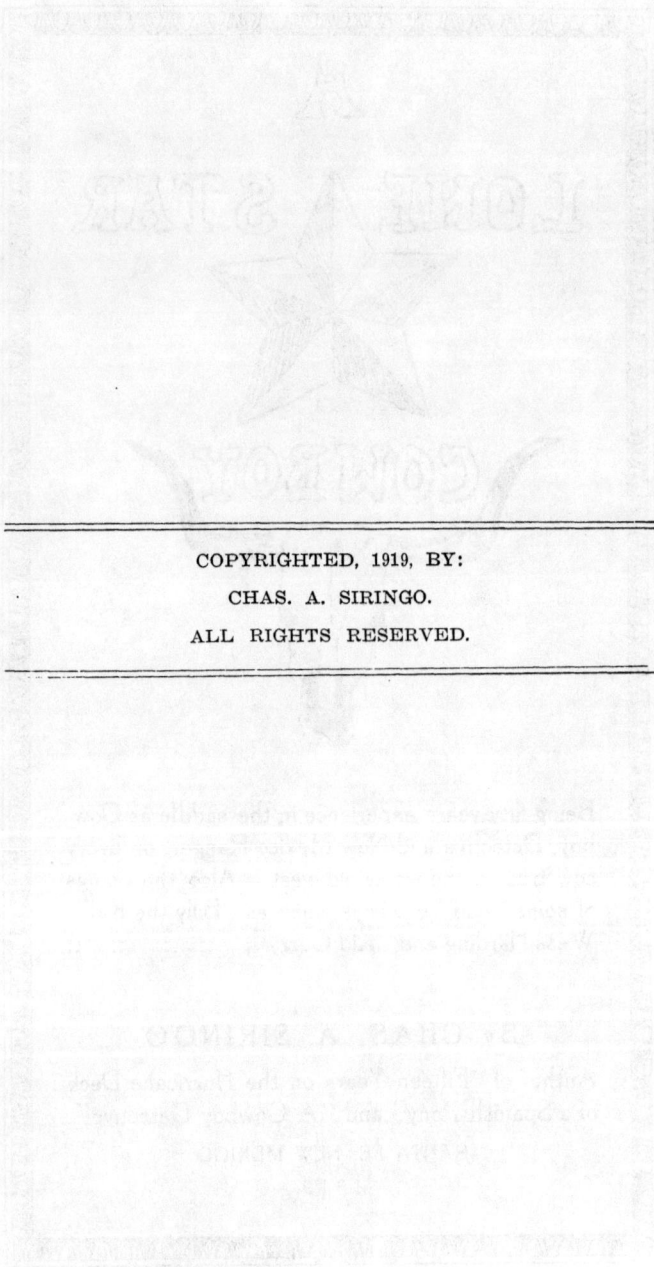

THE AUTHOR AND HIS RUSSIAN WOLF HOUND "JUMBO"

Dedicated to:

My broad-gauge friend, Alois B. Renehan, an
eminent lawyer of Santa Fe, New Mexico,
who is "a friend in need, as well as a friend
indeed."

The Author.

PREFACE

This volume is to take the place of "A Texas Cowboy," the copyright of which has expired. Since its first publication, in 1885, nearly a million copies have been sold. In this, "A Lone Star Cowboy," much cattle history is given which has never before been published.

CHAS. A. SIRINGO,
Santa Fe,
New Mexico.

LIST OF ILLUSTRATIONS

CONTENTS
CHAPTER I.
CHAPTER II.
CHAPTER III.
CHAPTER IV.
CHAPTER V.
CHAPTER VI.
CHAPTER VII.

CHAPTER I.

MY FIRST COWBOY EXPERIENCE.
TWO YEARS IN YANKEE-LAND, AND THE
CITY OF NEW ORLEANS

The writer was born and brought up amidst wild, long-horn cattle and mustangs in the ex· treme southern part of the Lone Star State.

I first saw the light of day, and had my first warm meal on the seventh day of February, 1855, in the county of Matagorda, Texas.

At the age of four I got my first book "larnin" from a "Yankee" school-master by the name of Hale. A year later war broke out between the North and South, and my beloved schoolmaster hiked north to join the Yankee army.

During the four years of bloody rebellion I saw much fighting on land and water, along the gulf coast, between the Federals and Confederates. Also saw many dead and wounded soldiers.

During the war our food consisted of fish, oysters, corn-bread and sweet potatoes. Coffee was made of parched corn and sweet potatoes.

When the cruel war was over, and I was eleven years of age, in the spring of 1867, I became a full-fledged Cowboy, wearing broad sombrero, high-

heeled boots, Mexican spurs, and the dignity of a
full-grown man. I had "hired out" to run cattle
for a Mr. Faldien, at a wage of ten dollars per
month. During the season our work was mostly
around Lake Austin, and on Bay prairie, where
now stands the thriving little city of Bay City.

The country was literally covered with wild
mustangs, and long-horn cattle. We did nothing
but round up and brand mavericks from one to
four years old, and I soon became handy with the
lasso, as these wild mavericks had to be lassoed,
thrown and branded with Mr. Faldien's brand.
The un-branded cattle were public property, and
our object was to "Make hay while the sun
shined" by putting Mr. Faldien's brand on as
many cattle as possible.

There were many other branding outfits in the
field, doing the same for themselves.

In 1868 my widowed mother married a "Yankee," and sold our home and cattle. The land
brought seventy-five cents an acre, and the cattle
one dollar a head. Then we boarded a Morgan
Steampship at Indianola, and started for Yankee-
dom by way of Galveston and New Orleans;
thence up the Mississippi River on a steamboat to
Saint Louis, Missouri, and by rail to Lebanon, St.
Clair County, Illinois, which I considered the
heart of Yankee-land.

Now the misery of a boy began. Having to
work out in the cold fields during the late winter

months, only half clothed, at a wage of eight dollars a month, which I never got the benefit of, as it went to buy whiskey for my drunken Yankee step-father;—but thank the stars, during spring he "hit the road" for parts unknown; then I drew the wages myself, as my Mother and only Sister went to St. Louis, Missouri, to try their luck in a strange city. That same Sister still lives in St. Louis, having married a prosperous business man. Four girls and one boy spring from that union, and most of them have families of their own, and are prosperous.

Mother and Sister had promised to write to me, giving their city address, but for some reason they failed to do so—hence a Texas long-horn Kid was left alone among strangers, and in a strange land.

During the summer I quit my heart-breaking job with Mr. Moore, and went to Lebanon to learn the carpenter trade. I had bound myself to an old skin-flint who was building a new dwelling for a Mr. Sargent, in the edge of town. He made me sign a contract that I would work for him three years to learn the trade.

I worked one whole day, from sun-up to sun-down, turning a grindstone to grind a lot of rusty tools. That night, by the light of the moon I walked twelve miles east, and next morning hired to a farmer with a heart, by the name of Jacobs, for twelve dollars a month.

During the harvest I made a half a hand binding and shocking wheat.

Late in the fall, 1869, I quit my job and walked to St. Louis, a distance of twenty-five miles, in hopes of finding Mother and Sister.

Little did I dream of the difficulty in finding two people in a city of nearly half a million souls.

No need to recite the hungry spells, and the hard beds on platforms and dry-goods boxes for two long weeks until I secured a job as bell-boy in the swell Planters Hotel.

My wages were ten dollars a month, but I averaged several dollars a day from tips. Often a crowd of gamblers playing for high stakes in a room would give me a ten or twenty dollar bill to buy a tray-load of drinks, telling me to keep the change.

The other dozen or more bell-boys did equally well in the way of easy tips, and when off duty we spent the money like drunken sailors.

One year later, in the fall of 1870, I had a rough and tumble fight with one of the bell-hops while on duty, and was slapped on the cheek by the chief clerk, Cunningham. This slapping stirred up the anger in my system, and I threw up the soft job of bell-boy.

With a few dollars in my pocket I started for the levee to board a steamboat headed toward Texas, but on the road to the levee I butted into a gambling game, and lost every cent of my money.

Late in the evening I stole my way onto the Bart Able, which was ready to steam down the Mississippi river for New Orleans, and hid among the freight sacks and boxes.

While loading freight from an old abandoned steamboat, in a town in Arkansas, I fell over backward into an open hatchway, about thirty feet deep and was fished out by the captain and crew more dead than alive.

On waking up I found myself in a clean bed in the captain's private room.

On reaching New Orleans I was able to walk but couldn't bend my back, and the back of my head had a lump on it the size of a cocoanut.

After eating a nice dinner on the Bart Able the boat steamed back up the river for St. Louis, leaving me in a strange city with not a cent in my pocket.

After two days of hunger, and sleeping on cotton bales, I was picked up by a kind hearted man, Wm. R. Myers, and taken to his lovely home, 18 Derbigny Street.

Mr. Myers was connected with the Couens Red River line of steamboats, and was wealthy in his own name.

After ringing the bell at the Myers fine home, Mrs. Mary P. Myers opened the door. She was evidently shocked at the sight of a dirty faced urchin at her husband's side. Mr. Myers introduced me as a young Texas "Hoosier" whom he bad brought home to fill up, as I was half starved.

The five o'clock dinner was ready to be served by the two negro servants, but bless you, I had to endure the agony of having the meal delayed until I could take a bath in the neat bath-room adjoining the dining room.

Don't wonder if my stomach was puffed out like a "Pizened pup" when dinner was over. It was, and the world appeared like one round ball of glory and contentment.

That night in the elegant parlor I was made tell my pedigree, and past life. The result was, this old couple who had no children, offered to adopt me as their own son, and to give me a fine education, with a start in business when twenty-one years of age.

Of course I consented, as the rosy picture of more juicy porterhouse steaks, broiled on a charcoal fire, loomed up in the future.

The next forenoon Mrs. Myers took me down to one of the swell clothing establishments and fitted me out like a young prince. I objected to the peaked toed gaiters and asked for a pair of star-top, high heeled boots, but the good lady thought boots would make me look too much like a "hoosier."

Seeing that she was lavish with her money, I asked her to buy me a violin, so that I could learn to play "The old blind mule came trotting through the wilderness," and other favorite Texas songs. This she agreed to do, and later carried out her promise.

After the crick in my back and the lump on my head had "vamoosed," in other words "flew the coop," and the rare beef-steaks had painted my cheeks with a rosy tint, I was sent to Fisk's Public School to start my education.

One week in school and I had a rough and tumble fight with another boy in the school room. In making my 'get-away' for the door, I ran over the good looking young teacher, Miss Finley, who was trying to prevent my escape. The poor girl fell flat on her back, and I stepped on her silk, pink-waist as I went over her for the door. No doubt she thought it was a Texas stampede.

A few days later I was sent to a pay school. This old professor only had a few select scholars, all boys, to whom he taught the German, French and English languages.

In the course of a few months I had to shake the dust of New Orleans from my peaked toed gaitors on account of stabbing one of the scholars with a pocket-knife. He was much larger than myself and had my face bloody.

Night found me wrapped in slumber among the cotton bales on board the Mollie Able, en-route to St. Louis. My slumber was not a peaceful one, as I awoke often to worry over my future, should the boy Steamcamp, die. I had seen the blood gushing from his wound as he ran screaming over the grassy lawn, where we had been playing during the afternoon recess.

On reaching St. Louis, after eight days and nights of hiding in the cotton bales, and stealing food after the deck hands finished their meals, I spent a day trying to find Mother and Sister. Then I crossed the river on a ferry boat and walked to Lebanon, Illinois, thence to the Jacobs farm, where I was received with open arms, and put to work in the harvest field, where I had worked the season previous.

When the harvest was over I longed for the easy life under Mrs. Myers' wing. Therefore I drew my wages and struck out afoot for St. Louis. I arrived there in time to board the Robert E. Lee, which was starting down the river on her great race with the Natchez. Thousands of dollars were bet on which one would reach New Orleans first.

I slipped onto the steamer and kept hidden most of the time when the captain, or the other officers were in sight. The cook kindly gave me food.

We landed in New Orleans ahead of the Natchez, and there was great rejoicing aboard. The citizens of New Orleans presented the captain with a pair of gold antlers to place on the bow of his swift steamer.

On the same evening of our arrival I hunted up Babe Fisher, a yellow negro whom I knew could be trusted, and who afterwards became a noted outlaw, to find out if the victim of my fight had recovered. I was informed that it required the skill of two prominent doctors to save young Steamcamp's life, but he was now about as sound as ever.

This encouraged me to ring the door bell at the Myers mansion. My dirty face was showered with kisses by Mrs. Myers, who was happy over my return. When Mr. Myers returned at night from his office, he too, gave me a hearty welcome.

Mr. Myers made three visits to the German professor before he could induce him to take me back as one of his pupils.

Now I took up my same old studies, German, French and English. I was a hero among the scholars for winning the fight with young Steamcamp, who had been the bully of the school. He had never returned to take up his studies after recovering.

Everything went on lovely, and I continued to enjoy the juicy beef-steaks which were served every evening, fresh from the charcoal furnace on the brick paved back yard.

In the latter part of November a big fire broke out near our school, and the street was lined with people going to the fire. I asked the professor if I could go and see the blaze. In a gruff voice he answered "No!" I then yelled "Goodbye," and broke for the door.

It was night when the excitement of the fire

died down. I then walked to the levee, and after
a wait of an hour or more I slipped onto the St.
Mary, a Morgan steamship bound for Indianola,
Texas.

I kept hid out all night, and next morning was
put to work scouring brass railings to pay for my
food and passage.

After a stormy trip we arrived in Indianola,
Texas, one morning about sun-up.

On viewing the old warf, from which I stepped
onto the gang-plank of the Crescent City about
two years previous, I shouted deep down in my
heart: Back at last to the dear Lone Star State;
the natural home of the cowboy and long-horn
steer.

The winter was spent working for H. Selickson,
in his beef factory, where cattle were butchered
for their hides and tallow; my wages being fifteen
dollars a month.

Early in the spring of 1871 I visited among my
friends in the town of Matagorda, and on the pen-
insula, the place of my birth.

About April the first I hired out to Tom Nie,
now known as "the Onion king" of Lerado, Texas.
He was making up a crew of cowboys to work on
the Rancho Grande, on Trespalacios Creek,
about twenty-five miles northwest from the town
of Matagorda.

We went by sail-boat to Palacios Point, where
the Rancho Grande Company had an outside

camp. There we joined other cowboys, making a crew of twenty, and from there went overland to the Rancho Grande headquarters

We found the headquarter ranch a busy place, getting ready for the spring work. Here there were a company store, a church house, and the nice home residence of Jonathan Pierce.

The two Pierce Brothers, Abel ("Shanghai") and Jonathan, were in partnership with Mr. Sam Allen, and a Mr. Pool, of eastern Texas. They owned this Rancho Grande, and the more than 100,000 long-horn cattle, scattered over hundreds of miles of grassy range.

There were about 50 cowboys at the headquarter ranch; a few Mexicans, and a few negroes among them. We had unlimited credit at the company store. My credit was stretched almost to the breaking point, in purchasing a cowboy outfit, such as saddle, bridle, spurs, pistol, bowie-knife, bedding, sombrero, silk handkerchiefs, slicker (rain coat), high-heel boots, etc.

"Shanghai" Pierce and his crew of cowboys had just arrived from the Rio Grande River with 300 wild Mexican ponies for the spring work. He had paid two dollars and fifty cents a head for them. They were what was termed "wet" ponies on the Rio Grande. In other words were stolen stock; hence the low prices.

On the Rio Grande river which separates Texas from Old Mexico, there were many traders in

"wet" ponies. A deal was made for any number of geldings put into the river on the Mexican
side. All those which swam over and landed on
the Texas side were paid for by the purchaser. Of
course they were still dripping with river water
when they climbed up the sandy bank on the
eastern shore of the river. Hence the term "wet"
ponies. They had been stolen by organized Mexican thieves from the large bands of Mexican ponies in Old Mexico. These wild ponies were divided among the three crews which started on the
Spring work in different directions.

Some of the boys were thrown from their bucking bronchos, but not so with the writer. I always
managed to stick on, even though the pony bucked
into the timber. Our camps were generally pitched
at the edge of a belt of timber; hence there was
great danger of being killed or crippled if the wild
pony went into the timber, instead of heading for
the open prairie.

We always started the day's work at the first
peep of day, and never thought of eating a noon
meal. Often it would be pitch dark when we arrived in camp, where a warm camp-fire meal
awaited us. These meals were made up of meat
from a fat heifer calf, with corn bread, molasses,
and black coffee. The negro cook, who drove the
mess-wagon, generally had two kinds of meat, the
calf ribs broiled before the camp fire, and a large

dutch oven full of loin, sweet-breads, and heart, mixed with flour gravy.

For breakfast we often had pork and beans which had been simmering over hot coals all night. In those days knives and forks were seldom used in the cow-camps; each cowboy used his bowie-knife or pocket knife to eat with. Nor were there tents to sleep in when it rained. The boys slept on the ground, covered with a canvas or wagon-sheet to turn the water.

The crew of which I was a member consisted of fifteen men and boys. We started work on the Navidad River, in Jackson County, gathering a herd of eleven hundred head of steers for Mr. Black, who had brought his crew of green Kansas boys, overland from Wichita, Kansas.

In gathering this herd of old "Mossy horn" steers, from four to twenty years old, I had a new experience. They were mostly wild timber cattle, which only graze out in the edges of the prairies at night, going back to the timber after daylight. We had to make raids on them before sun-up, by which time they would be back in the brushy timber, where it was impossible to round them up, or rope and tie down the unruly ones.

It is hard to believe, but nevertheless true, that some of these old steers had a fine coating of moss on their long horns. The trees were all covered with moss; some more than a foot long.

By the time we got this herd "put up," and

turned over to Mr. Black and his crew, we were a
worn out bunch of cowboys. Every steer had to
be roped and thrown to be road-branded, and we
had to stand guard every night, half the crew the
first part of the night and the balance until daylight. During rain and thunder storms every cowboy had to be in the saddle all night, singing and
whistling to the restless cattle to avoid a stampede. At such times there was no sleep for any
one but the cook.

Stampedes were frequent on stormy nights, and
we had to stay with the running herd until the
steers became exhausted.

It was said that Mr. Black and his crew lost the
whole herd, through stampedes and mixing up
with the wild range cattle, before reaching Red
River, on the line of the Indian "Nation," now
Oklahoma. Later "Shanghai" Pierce reported
meeting Mr. Black in Wichita, Kansas, working at his trade of blacksmithing. He said that his
first experience with long-horns had left him a
financial wreck.

The balance of the season, up to Christmas, we
put in our time branding mavericks and calves.
The mavericks were not as plentiful, or as old, as
when I took my first lessons as a cowboy in 1867.
Among the timber cattle we found some unbrand-
ed bulls and cows, four and five years old, but on
the prairies they ranged from one to two years of

age, being calves which escaped the branding iron the previous seasons.

During this year of 1871 the Rancho Grande company branded 25,000 calves and mavericks.

I finally wrote to Mr. and Mrs. Myers in New Orleans telling them that I had attained the desire of my life by becoming a full-fledged cowboy, in the Lone Star State. In a few weeks an answer was received to my letter. In it was a twenty dollar bill, and a pass on the Morgan steamship Line from Indianola to New Orleans, the money being for my expenses en route.

In the letter they begged me to return and finish my education. I wrote them that the life of a cowboy was good enough for me, and offered to return the money and the pass. In a later letter Mr. Myers wrote me to tear up the pass, and to buy a suit of clothes with the twenty dollar "william." Many years later this old couple died, and were buried in the town of Pocatello, Idaho. Mr. Myers had lost his wealth in a bad speculation with a thieving partner in Florida. Before old age put them under the sod, I had the pleasure of repaying them for all the money spent on me when a wild, reckless lad.

Mrs. Myers had a sister, Mrs. Henry Beecraft, living in Pocatello, Idaho, and she saw that they had a decent burial.

Such is life. I often think of what a narrow

escape I had of becoming an educated business man, had I remained in New Orleans.

After the branding season was over I joined "Bob" Partain's crew, and we established winter quarters at the camp house three miles from Palacios Point. Our work was shipping steers to New Orleans and Cuba. Twice a week a Morgan steamship would tie up at the wharf at Palacios Point, and it was our duty to put about five hundred cattle aboard.

Gathering crews would deliver the steers to our outfit, and we had to night-herd them until ready to ship.

During cold northers and sleet storms we had a tough job night-herding. Often "Shanghai" Pierce would be present to help us sing to the cattle during bad storms. "Shanghai" felt at home on the back of a pony. Quite different from his brother Jonathan, who was never so happy as when plowing with a yoke of oxen. In all the years that I knew Jonathan I never saw him in a saddle.

It often happened that we wouldn't get the steers aboard the ship until late at night. Then we would fill up on George Burkhart's cowboy's delight, such as peaches and brandy, cherries and brandy, and Hostetter's bitters.

No other kind of liquors were kept in the store. On leaving the little village we would shoot off our pistols, and make a mad race of three miles for the camp house. Often several saddled ponies would be waiting for the morning feed of corn at the corral, their drunken riders having fallen by the wayside in the race for camp.

When spring came I was assigned with a new crew in charge of Mr. Wiley Kuykendall, who had married a sister of the Pierce brothers.

It is said that strong coffee and tobacco will kill a man. If this were true Mr. Kuykendall would have been in his grave long ago instead of leading a happy, retired life in Victoria, Texas, at the present time.

"Mr. Wiley," as we cowboys affectionately called him, spent a very little of his time in bed. He was fond of black coffee, steaming hot from the camp coffee pot, and only when asleep did the smoke from his black pipe cease. He was up with the cook every morning, so as to get his cup of hot coffee.

When time to wake the sleeping cowboys for breakfast, "Mr. Wiley" would go out to where their beds were spread on the ground, and shout: "Come boys, come, get up and hear the little birds singing their sweet praises to God Almighty; D—n your souls, get up!" The first part of the sentence was in a sweet, low, tender voice, while the last part was in a loud, angry tone. This was an every morning occurence while I worked with him.

A few years previous to the writing of this, I visited with Mr. and Mrs. Kuykendall at a swell

hotel in Hot Springs, Arkansas, and found "Mr.
Wiley" a healthy old man, still wearing his cowboy hat, boots and red, silk sash to keep his pants
up, in lieu of suspenders. Of course he attracted
much attention among the hotel guests, but he
didn't seem to realize it. He had become wealthy
through the rise in the value of long-horn cattle
and Texas soil.

While in Hot Springs, Mr. Kuykendall "harked
back" to his barefoot days, when, as an orphan
boy, in 1866, the year after the rebellion, he helped
drive one of the first herds of long-horn steers
"up the trail" to Kansas and Missouri.

The cattle were owned by a Mr. Herindon, on
the Colorado River, in Matagorda County. They
started early in the spring, driving the herd in a
haphazard way toward the north, as there was no
trail to follow.

They crossed the south-east corner of Kansas,
at Baxter Springs, and entered Missouri, where
the steers were sold. Then Mr. Kuykendall says
he and other cowboys started for home, overland,
with the ramutha, (saddle ponies) and pack outfit, on which the grub and bedding were carried.
In Missouri one of the pack mules was loaded
down with apples, on which the men partially sub-
sisted until reaching home just before Christmas.

I shall always hold the name of "Mr. Wiley" in
kind remembrance, as in the summer of 1872 he
gave me my first start in the cattle business, by

allowing me to put my own brand, which had not yet been recorded, as the law required, on a few mavericks. This made me bold, so that thereafter I always carried a rod of iron tied to my saddle, as a branding iron, to be made red hot in a brush, or "cow-chip" fire, when riding over the prairie alone, and a fine looking maverick showed up. The short piece of iron being bent at one end and used to "run" my brand on the animal's hip.

In the late summer our crew was sent to Lavaca and Calhoun Counties to gather steers and ship them on board Morgan steamships, in Indianola, for the New Orleans market.

Later we were sent to Wharton and Colorado Counties to gather steers to be shipped by rail from Richmond and Houston.

It was while driving a herd of these fat steers to Richmond that I was bitten on the foot by a rattlesnake, which proves that even the bite of a snake can't kill a tough cowboy.

We had just swam the herd across a swollen stream, which caused me to get wet to the skin. While I was guarding the herd, part of the crew having gone to dinner, I disrobed to let my clothes dry in the hot sun. While standing barefooted in the tall grass the snake put two gashes across one foot.

This caused the death of his snakeship, as I was angry and beat him to a pulp. My foot and leg became badly swollen, so that I couldn't wear my left boot for a week; still I never missed doing my full share of the work, which included standing guard over the herd half of each night.

During the fall "Mr. Wiley" severed his connection with the outfit, and soon after I did likewise.

I had been working for the Rancho Grande Company nearly two years, without a settlement, or knowing how my account in the company store stood. My wages were twenty dollars a month, and whenever I needed cash, all I had to do was ask old "Hunkey Dorey" Brown, who was in charge of the store, for the amount, and he would charge it on my account. I was a surprised and disappointed boy when I found that I only had seventy-five cents to my credit. This I "blowed in" for a bottle of peaches and brandy, and some stick candy, before leaving the store to ride away on my own pony.

CHAPTER II

SHOT AND WOUNDED IN THE KNEE
A STRUGGLE FOR LIFE IN A GREAT STORM ON THE GULF COAST OF TEXAS

At the time Mr. Wiley Kuykendall quit the firm, the Pierce Brothers had sold their cattle interests to Allen and Pool for the snug sum of $110,000, which was a fortune in those days.

This shows what men with Yankee blood in their veins could do with long-horn cattle.

As a young man, before the Rebellion, "Shanghai" Pierce had drifted from the state where they make wooden nutmegs and went to work for W. B. Grimes, on Tres Palacios Creek, splitting live-oak rails at a wage of one dollar a day.

In later years Mr. Pierce used to point out this old rail fence, which he put up, as the folly of his youth.

Late in the fall the Rancho Grande headquarters was established at Mr. John Moore's ranch home, at the mouth of Tres Palacios Creek—Mr. Moore being appointed general manager.

John Moore had an only son, Bennie, who was put in charge of a crew to ride over the prairies to cut off the horns of old stray bulls—that is animals which had no recorded owner, as they had drifted with the hordes of other cattle during northers and sleet storms from the north, during the four years of bloody Rebellion, when the men and boys of middle and northern Texas were too busy fighting the Yankees to look after their cattle.

During the late fall much of my time was spent with Bennie Moore's crew helping rope and throw these wild bulls. It was fun for me, and I asked no pay.

Bennie Moore was champion bull roper of the crew. He had two ponies gored to death by angry bulls, tied to one end of a thirty foot rope, the other end being securely fastened to the saddle horn, which was the custom in those days.

These lassos were made of either hard twisted grass, rawhide, or hair from a horses mane.

The cowboy who was first to throw his rope over the bulls head would run around him while he was on the run, and when his front legs were over the rope Mr. Bull would flop over, then one of the boys would pitch his rope onto one or both hind legs and stretch him out. Now a man with a sharp axe would slash off half the horn which rested on the ground. Then he was turned over and the other horn cut off. Now the bloody old brute was turned loose to ponder over the cruelties of man.

The object of cutting off the horns was to prevent goring each other while on board of a ship.

Soon after, poor Bennie Moore was struck and killed by lightning, leaving two young sons, who are now prosperous cattlemen at Uvalde, Texas.

Previous to selling out to Allen and Pool "Shanghai" Pierce had made a contract with the Cuban Government to furnish them 100,000 head of bulls to feed their soldier boys.

Before quitting the Rancho Grande Company I had helped put some of those bulls on board the Morgan Steamships. For some reason only part of this great number of bulls were ever shipped. No doubt the soldiers rebelled, and swore off eating bull-beef.

For many years afterwards these old bulls with both horns chopped off could be seen leading a contented life on the grassy prairies of Colorado, Wharton, Jackson and Matagorda Counties.

During the winter of 1873 and 74 some of these old bulls put easy money into my own pocket.

Their hides were worth five dollars each, when dried. As they were strays I considered it no sin to kill and skin them. I would ride up close to the bull and plant a bullet from my powder and ball, Colts pistol behind his ear.

During the winter of 1872-73 I made my home at the Horace Yeamans ranch on Cashes Creek. Old man Yeamans had a son, Horace, about my own age, and we went into partnership skinning "dead" cattle. They died that winter by the tens of thousands all over this coast country, bordering the bay of Matagorda. The country had become overstocked through the natural increase, and the hordes which drifted from the north during cold northers and sleet storms. Often a boggy slough would be completely bridged over with dead and dying cattle, so that the ones following could walk over dry-footed.

Horace and I did most of our skinning that winter at Hamitlon's Point where the little city of Palacios now stands. Here the famished brutes

could go no further south on account of Tres Palacios Bay—hence they died by the thousands.

We made "Big" money all winter. As a side
issue I had put my brand on a lot of mavericks
during spare times.

In the spring my brand was sold to George
Hamilton, he paying me two dollars a head for all
cattle in my brand, gathered by the different
branding outfits during the coming seasons. The
last money he paid me was in 1879—Several years
after making the trade.

Now I had a new brand recorded in Matagorda,
the County Seat, to put on other mavericks. I had
the foresight to select a stray brand, which I knew
was not on record—hence had no owner. I had
seen grown cattle in this brand. The chances were
that this brand belonged in one of the northern
Counties of the state.

The first money received from this new brand
was for a twelve or fifteen year old steer which I
found in W. B. Grimes' slaughter pen ready to be
butchered for his hide and tallow.

Never shall I forget the look on old man Grimes'
face when I demanded ten dollars for this steer.
He couldn't understand how a smooth face boy
could have the gall to claim such an old animal, on
the strength of a new brand only on record a few
months. Showing him the recorders certificate
convinced this shrewd old Yankee that I was the

rightful owner. He paid me for a few others later.

In this hide and tallow factory Mr. Grimes slaughtered from one to three hundred head of cattle a day—many of them being strays, which didn't cost him a cent.

During the late fall Horace Yeamans and I made a camping trip along the Bay shore to lay in a supply of bacon for the winter. The marshes were full of wild hogs. We only killed fat sows.

When the skinning season was over, in the spring, I hired out at twenty dollars a month to Mr. W. B. Grimes. My job—along with other cowboys—was to guard the slaughter-pen herd until ready to be butchered. Mr. Nolan Keller was in charge of the gathering crew. About twice a week he would arrive with several hundred head of steers and turn them over to our crew.

In the late spring Mr. Grimes gave me charge of his range stock of horses. I had to attend the horse roundups in Matagorda, Wharton, Colorado and Jackson counties to brand up the W. B. G. colts.

When the branding season was over I took a contract to break some wild ponies at two dollars and fifty cents a head.

Some days I would ride as high as five head of these wild ponies, which had never been saddled before. Most of them were vicious buckers. They had to be roped and thrown in order to get the hackamore—a rope halter—and the leather blind onto them.

When the animal was allowed to get up on his feet, his eyes being blinded, he always stood quite still until the saddle was fastened on his back. Then the blind was raised in order to allow him to wear himself out bucking around the corral with the saddle.

Now he was put outside the corral, and the leather blind lowered back over his eyes. Then when seated in the saddle the blind was raised, and the bucking and running began. It often required two hours time to get him docile and back to the corral. Then he was turned loose among the others in the corral, and a fresh one saddled.

I had no help in this work. In those days a cowboy considered it a disgrace to have help in saddling and managing a wild broncho.

Now, in these later years, a broncho-buster nearly always has a helper to get the saddle on the broncho's back and to guide him over the prairie.

After I had ridden each of these ponies about a dozen times—the last few times with a bridle-bit in his mouth—they were turned over to the owner as ''broke.''

The winter was spent with Horace Yeamans in the skinning of ''dead'' cattle, and the branding of mavericks during spare times.

By this time I was old enough to begin to feel my oats—as a horsetrainer would say about his racer. Therefore I attended many dances during the winter—some of them twenty-five miles distant from the Yeaman's ranch.

One day when ready to ride away to one of these distant dances, in company with Miss Sallie Yeamans, I thought seriously of heaven and hell while being dragged over the prairie by a wild broncho.

The proper way to mount a skittish horse is to pull his head around towards you with the left arm and grab the saddle-horn with the right hand, then put your foot in the stirrup.

This I failed to do in mounting Satan—a large sorrel broncho.

My number five high-heel, star-top, boot was shoved into the stirrup before grabbing the saddle-horn. The result was Satan went to bucking and I fell over backwards with my left foot hung in the stirrup.

The long hackmore rope, fastened to Satan's nose, had been held coiled up in my left hand. It fell to the ground, and while being dragged on my back I could see a negro cowboy, who was present, running his best, afoot, trying to catch the end of the rope. At one time he was within a few feet of the dragging rope. Then I felt hopeful. But when I saw the end of the rope crawling further away from the negro, I lost hope, and began to wonder what kind of a place hell was, and whether I would be treated with kindness.

After a few hundred yards of dragging, with Satan's hind hoofs flying over my up-turned face, I began to kick frantically with my left leg. This brought the foot out of the stirrup.

As the end of the hackamore rope went past me I grabbed it and hung on like grim death to a dead nigger. Now I was dragging on my stomach, which wore the bosom of my white "Stake and rider, Sunday-go-to-meetin'" shirt into a frazzle. I finally had to turn the rope loose.

This was certainly a case of being dragged to hell by Satan, had my foot not come out of the stirrup.

Satan was found with a wild bunch of ponies a month or two later, still wearing the saddle on his back.

I finally sold him cheap to a drunken Irishman by the name of Martin. He and Dan—another gentleman from the "ould sod"—were building dirt dams to hold stock water for the Rancho Grande Company. I had Satan pretty tame when sold to Martin. But next morning Martin was quite sober and concluded to give his pony a little training. Their camp was located in the timber near a narrow road.

Martin mounted the pony and told Dan to go a short distance up the road and hide behind a pile of brush, then when he came galloping by, to suddenly spring out of the brush. He said he wanted to get the pony trained to not scare at strange objects.

When Dan picked Martin up with a skinned face and body he swore at Dan for scaring the pony too hard. Said he ought to have sprung out of the brush easy. This was Martin's last ride on Satin—as he joined a wild bunch away from the haunts of dam-builders.

Early in the coming spring I hired out to Tom Merril (who was later murdered, as was also his young wife, by renegade Mexicans in Tom Green County, Texas), at thirty-five dollars a month, to be one of his cowboys "up the Chisholm Trail" to Kansas.

We gathered and road-branded the herd of old "mossy-horn" steers, eleven hundred head, on the Navidad River in Jackson County.

These steers were purchased from Leandro and Lafe Ward by the Mackelroy Brothers, who had hired Mr. Merrill to boss the herd "up the Chisholm Trail."

Before reaching Austin, the Capital City of Texas, I rebelled on account of having to break wild ponies for other cowboys who were poor riders.

Henry Coats—now a prosperous resident of Jackson County—and I had to do all the bronchobusting.

Later Henry Coats also rebelled and quit the outfit.

On reaching my stamping ground in Matagorda County I worked for "Daddy" Grimes a while, then pulled off many other stunts, too numerous to mention.

During the coming winter I established a camp out in the open, at the head of Cashes Creek, and put in my time skinning "dead" cattle and branding mavericks.

The old brand which I had on record had been sold, along with all cattle wearing it. Hence I recorded a new brand, T5 connected, to put on the new crop of mavericks.

Later this brand, and the cattle were sold to Fred Cornelius, now a wealthy cattleman of Midfield, Texas, a town which sprang up on the ground where much of my mavericking was done.

During all these more than forty years, up to date, Fred Cornelius has used this T5 brand on his thousands of cattle, which he has owned since buying the brand in 1875.

When spring came I was put out of active business. I was seated on the ground by the campfire smoking, late in the evening, when Sam Grant, a "nigger" killer, rode up and dismounted. Picking up my pistol, which lay on the opposite side of the fire from where I was sitting, he examined it, then threw it away, at the same time pulling his pistol, with the remark, "Why don't you have a good one like mine!" He then fired at my heart.

My hands were clamped around my left leg—the knee being on a level with my heart. The large dragoon bullet struck the knee going through and lodging near the skin on the opposite side.

He was raising the pistol as though to fire again when a negro cowboy, Lige, galloped into camp out of the heavy timber and brush. This, no doubt, saved my life.

Grant swore to Lige, who had dismounted, and was holding me up with one hand, that his pistol went off accidentally.

Then Grant galloped away saying he would send a doctor from Demings Bridge Post-office, the old Rancho Grande Headquarters.

The doctor came late at night and cut the bullet out. Lige assisted me to the Yeamans ranch a few miles below on the creek.

It was thirty-five years later when I learned from my friend Nolan Keller, the true secret of this attempted assassination.

A certain wealthy cattleman, who is now dead, hired Sam Grant to kill me, on account of my boldness in branding mavericks, and killing stray bulls for their hides.

At that time Nolan Keller was foreman for this cattle-man and learned the secret of his deal with Grant.

Mr. Keller is now a respected citizen of Palacios, Texas.

When able to ride, and walk with a crutch, I

made my home with Mr. John Pierce at the old
Rancho Grande headquarters. All I had to do was
assist little Johnny Pierce—now a wealthy banker
of Palacios, Texas,—and "Shanghai" Pierce's
little daughter, Mamie, to and from the school
house, two miles distant.

It was my duty to care for their ponies and to
see that the youngsters were not hurt. At the
same time I was getting some book learning, by
attending school myself. I found it a pleasant
home at the Pierce residence. Mrs. Nanny Pierce
and her old mother, Mrs. Lacy, were like mothers
to me.

The old lady, Mrs. Lacy, used to "hark back,"
and tell me of my Grand-parents, the Whites, who
in 1852, bought a tract of land from the Lacys, on
Tres Palacios Creek.

She told of how the Whites built a nice farm
house with the first glass windows ever seen in
that part of the state. They had brought the glass
from Ireland with them.

In the family there were three husky boys, and
two girls—my mother being one of the girls.

The boys built a sod fence around their field—
the outlines of which can still be traced.

Mrs. Lacy told of how the great storm of 1854
scattered the White residence over the prairie,
leaving pieces of window glass on its path.

This calamity broke the old couple's hearts, and
they soon after died in the log house built after

the storm. Their bodies were laid to rest at the foot of an old live-oak tree, by the Lacy family and other neighbors.

A few weeks after starting to school the red-headed schoolmaster, Mr. Carson, concluded to whip me, so as to convince the other scholars that he wore men's size pants, but when he started in I pulled a knife and threated to carve him into mince-meat if he didn't go back and sit down, which he did.

I remained until school was dismissed, so as to take the Pierce children home. Next morning I saddled my pony, bade the Pierces goodby, and headed east with my crutch tied to the saddle.

At the Sam Allen ranch on Simms Bayou I laid over a few days to rest. Mr. Sam Allen, for whom I had worked when he was in partnership with the Pierce brothers, treated me royally. He was a fine old man, but at meals he wouldn't allow his cowboys to cut bread from the loaf. He said it was bad luck. It had to be broken.

I often wonder if his son, who has stepped into the old man's boots since his death, and who is at this writing, a wealthy resident of Houston, still keeps up the superstition.

While visiting my aunt Mary McClain, of Houston, and Uncle Nicholas White, of Galveston, I had the pleasure of shaking hands with the Confederate President, Jeff Davis. While attending the first State Fair ever held in Texas, at Houston, Uncle "Nick," who was an old confederate soldier, introduced me to Mr. Davis.

On leaving Galveston Uncle "Nick" slipped some "green-back" money into my pocket, and presented me with the old Spencer repeating rifle which he had carried through the civil war; he said it had put many Yankees to sleep. Of course I was proud of the gift, as cartridge repeating rifles were scarce, and hard to obtain in those days.

Another stop at the Sam Allen ranch, and then I hired out to Joe Davis, who had a contract furnishing beef to the building crews on the Gulf, Colorado, and Santa Fe railroad at Virginia Point, near Galveston.

Early in the fall I landed back at Demings Bridge post-office, and learned that Mother was waiting for me at the Morris ranch at Hamiltons Point.

On getting my letter in St. Louis, Missouri, telling of my wound, she hurried to me, but arrived only a few days after I had departed for parts unknown to anyone, hence she had a long and anxious wait.

It was September when I found Mother sick in bed at the Morris home.

As Mr. Morris, and his son Tom, were going to Indianola in their schooner, Mother and I scraped together all the cash we had and sent after lumber, etc., to build a home. But this money went to feed the fishes in Matagorda Bay, as the great storm of 1875, which washed Indianola off the face of the earth, scattered the Morris schooner, and everything on board, to the four winds of heaven. Morris and his son saved themselves by swimming.

This same storm cured Mother of her sickness. About ten o'clock at night, when the seventy-five mile wind took the roof off the Morris house, letting in the flood of rain, I picked Mother up out of her sick bed and jumped into the foaming water, which was more than waist deep.

Through my advice Mrs. Morris and her two little girls and two sons followed suit. It required all my strength to hang onto Mother and to keep the Morris family from drowning. Once they became tangled up in a bunch and were on top of Jimmie, the oldest boy, who was under the water.

The wind was from the west, blowing us out into Tres Palacios bay—two miles wide.

Knowing that there was an osage hedge of large trees a few hundred yards to the westward, I decided to face the wind and tide to reach that haven of safety. Hence my little crew were drilled to keep only their heads above water and their feet in the mud—leaning their bodies towards the wind.

All except Mother, who was as limber as a dishrag, heeded my advise. .

Inch by inch we crept towards the hedge. It required nearly an hour's struggle to reach it. Then we were saved.

When daylight came the only living creature, outside of ourselves, in sight, was a bay broncho which Jimmie and I had caught from a wild bunch the evening before. He was tied at the end of a long rope fastened to a strong stake driven into the ground. He had been floundering in water almost over his back during the night, but now it was only knee deep—as the tide was going down.

By looking across the bay we could see the shore piled high with rubbish and dead stock.

When the sun peeped over the eastern horizon we began to think of breakfast. The nearest ranch was the Yeamans home, five miles to the northward.

Jimmie, who was younger than myself, and I decided to draw straws to see who should ride the wild broncho bare-back to the Yeamans ranch after a wagon and grub. Jimmie drew the unlucky straw.

We used a shirt to make a blind for the broncho. When Jimmie was seated on his bare back, with the hackamore reins in his hands, I raised the blind and said "go." We had made a hackamore out of the stake rope that the broncho was tied with.

In spite of the hard bucking, Jimmie stuck on his back, and finally got him headed north in a run.

It was noon when the wagon and grub arrived.

Strange to relate, this ducking cured Mother and she forgot about being sick.

She lived to be eighty-six years of age and died a peaceful death in the Sister's Sanitarium in New Mexico's Capital City, Santa Fe.

With almost her last breath she begged me to make my peace with God, while the making was good.

Five years have passed since that dear old mother was laid away in Rosario Cemetery.

I have been too busy to heed her last advice. Being a just God, I feel that He will overlook my neglect. If not, I will have to take my medicine, with Satan holding the spoon.

CHAPTER III.

A TRIP UP THE CHISHOLM TRAIL TO KANSAS. A LONELY RIDE THROUGH THE INDIAN NATION.

In the early spring of 1876 I hired out to W. B. Grimes to help drive a herd "Up the Chisholm Trail" to Kansas, at thirty dollars a month.

We gathered the herd of 2500 old "mossyhorn" steers on the Navidad and Guadalupe rivers, in Colorado, Jackson and Victoria Counties.

None but old steers, from five to twenty years old were gathered. Most of them were wild timber cattle which only venture out on the edges of the prairies at night—grazing back to the timber before sunup.

At first, while the herd was small, we would corral at night in one of the many public corrals scattered over this coast country. When the herd become too large, we had to night-herd, each cowboy being up singing to the steers half the night.

In corraling these steers for the night we had great sport. Often we wouldn't get to camp with the bunch gathered that day until after dark. In that case the job of getting the whole herd into the corral was a severe one.

These public corrals, built of large live-oak logs, had wings extending out from the gate several hundred yards; the outer ends of the wings being far apart.

We would handle the herd gently until inside the wing enclosure, then a man up a tree would think Hades had broken loose. Then it became a case of shove. The yelling and beating of quirts against leather "chaps" could be heard miles away.

We were lucky to get half the herd into the corral the first attempt. Then the ones which had broken through the string of yelling cowboys were rounded up, and another attempt made.

Towards the last there would be many old fighting steers which couldn't be got back to the wing enclosures. Some would run for the timber near by, fighting mad. Then there was nothing to do but tie the mad brute down till morning. This being a dangerous job for a lone cowboy if the night was dark.

For the purpose of tying down these unruly steers pieces of hobble rope were kept tied on the saddles.

One dark night I ran out of rope hobbles—having previously tied down three steers—and had to tie a mad brute down with my silk sash—used wrapped around my waist to keep up my pants, in place of suspenders. I could have tied him down with his own tail, but that way of tying an animal generally lames one leg for a few days.

In tying a cow-brute down with its own tail, the hair on the end of the tail is divided into equal parts, then knotted together at the ends, forming a loop. Now the tail is wound once or twice around the animal's upper hind leg while lying flat on the ground, and the loop put between the split hoof. This keeps that leg drawn up so that the animal can not stand on its feet very long at a time.

It was against the rules to hog-tie a trail steer, as it caused stiffness in the legs. Only the two hinds legs were tied together, which allowed the animal to stand up, though he couldn't travel very far in that condition.

Sometimes we had to sew up the eye-lids of these old "Mossy-horn" steers to prevent them running for the timber every chance they got. It required about two weeks time to rot the thread, allowing the eyes to open. By this time the animal was "broke in."

After gathering the herd of 2500 steers the job of road-branding began. Small bunches were cut off from the main herd and put in a corral. Then each animal had to be roped and thrown by cowboys afoot, who worked in pairs. Now the road-brand, G, was burnt into the hair sufficiently deep to last "up the trail."

Often the corral was ankle deep with mud, making it tough on the cowboy's fine, calf-skin boots. Being wet they were hard to get off and on, therefore the boys generally slept with their boots on. At one time I wore my boots night and day for two weeks at a stretch, as they were number fives when they should have been number sixes. Cowboys took great pride in small feet.

When we finally got strung out "up the trail" the crew consisted of twenty-five cowboys, the cook,who drove the mess-wagon, and the boss, Asa Dowdy.

Stampedes at night during the spring rains and thunder storms were frequent. Then the boys had to remain in the saddle all night, otherwise they could sleep half the night.

The striking of a match to light a cigarette, or pipe, or a pony shaking the saddle, often caused stampedes.

On reaching the town of Gonzales our boss did

a foolish thing. He concluded to give the boys a full nights rest by corraling the whole herd in the large House corral, a few miles west of town.

By night we had the whole herd into the corral. It was jammed full.

After supper, as was the custom when a corral contained wild cattle, all the boys took their bedding and night-horse to the corral and spread out their beds around it, equal distances apart.

Then the boys retired for the night, sleeping with their clothes on, and holding the bridle-reins, or hackamore rope, of their pony in one hand.

These public corrals were built round, so that in case of a stampede, the boys could, by yelling and the shaking of slickers, etc., get the herd to milling in a circle, until exhausted.

About midnight while we were all asleep, a storm sprang up. A loud crash of thunder and lightning started a stampede. The frightened herd went through the corral where I was sleeping. I barely had time to mount my pony, which saved me from being trampled to death.

The corral was built of large live-oak logs and rails—the largest logs being at the bottom, next to the ground. The herd went through it as though it was built of paper.

While running in the lead of the herd, during flashes of lightning, I could see fence rails on top of the steers backs. The herd being jammed into a solid mass the rails couldn't fall to the ground.

The boss had slept in camp with his clothes off. In this condition he sprang onto his night-horse, tied to a wagon wheel, and was soon in the lead of the herd; but before getting there his pony ran against a tree and almost tore off one of his little toes, he being fare-footed. Being in his under clothes he suffered greatly from the wound, and cold rain. At daylight I tied up the wound with a handkerchief. The toe was hanging by the strong cords. I managed to get it back in place before tying it up.

On reaching the edge of the prarie, about a mile from camp, the herd split in two halves, the boss and I staying with one bunch.

When daylight came, and the steers had exhaust ed themselves, we were ten miles from camp, on an open prairie.

On riding back to camp over the trail made by the fleeing herd in the soft mud, many steers with broken legs were passed. Some had one or both horns knocked loose from their heads. This being caused by running up against the corral, or into trees before reaching the prairie.

I doubt if there ever was such a large herd of wild steers put into one corral before, or since.

On reaching the Capital city of Austin, on the Colorado River, two hundred miles from its mouth at the town of Matagordo, we struck the "Chisholm Trail" proper. From here north to the line of Kansas, a distance of about seven hundred

miles, it was one continuous road-way, several
hundred yards wide, tramped hard and solid by
the millions of hoofs which had gone over it. It
started in at a ford three miles below the city. All
smaller trails from the different Gulf-coast dis-
tricts merged into this great and only ''Chisholm
Trail.''

Now half of our crew returned home overland,
leaving us with a crew of twelve cowboys, with six
picked ponies for each rider.

We finally reached the over-grown county seat
of Ft. Worth—now one of the leading cities of
Texas. We drove through the eastern edge of
town covered with new board shanties. Dogs running out to bark at us caused a stampede. The
occupants of these new houses became greatly excited until the running herd was past.

Ft. Worth's first railroad, the Texas Pacific,
had just struck town, or was near by, which ac-
counted for so many new houses on the old ''Chisholm Trail.''

After leaving Ft. Worth we found many of the
watering places fenced up by new settlers. Barbed
wire had just come into use, and many of the
fences were of this material. We paid no attention
to fences, but shoved the herd right through them.

On one occasion we had a big stampede when
the barbed wire hung to the steers horns and
tails, and the big and little ''hoe-men'' ran out to
sick the dogs on us. Some of these dogs ''bit the

dust'' by having hot lead shot into them by angry
cowboys, who regarded the ''Chisholm Trail'' too
sacred to be scratched with plows and hoes.

We passed through a ten mile stretch of blackjack timber before reaching Red River, the dividing line between Texas and the Indian ''Nation,''
now the state of Oklahoma.

We found Red River a raging torrent, nearly a
mile wide, and full of drifting trees and logs.
Therefore we were compelled to ''lay over'' a couple of days to wait for the river to lower, as the
drifting timber made it too dangerous to attempt
a crossing.

There were about twenty herds ahead of us
waiting for the driftwood to cease flowing.

These twenty-one camps were about half a mile
apart, and at night the air rang with the voices of
singing cowboys. These songs were mostly old
favorites, such as Sam Bass, Mustang Grey, The
Dying Cowboy, and When You and I Were Young
Maggie.

The next day other herds arrived, which swelled
the numbers of camps, all within a radius of a few
miles.

On the evening of the second day the Cattle Inspector from Red River Station, a few miles up
the river, visited all the camps and told the bosses
that he would start in early next morning to inspect the herds. He was employed by the state to
inspect all cattle before they crossed the river

into the Indian "Nation." His fee was ten cents a head, and it was his duty to cut out all strays not wearing the regular road-brand. Range cattle were scattered all along the trail and many of them would get into the herds while spread out grazing.

At daylight the following morning the Inspector rode into the nearest camp to the crossing to inspect that herd.

The boys were eating breakfast and the boss invited the Inspector to have a cup of coffee.

While drinking the coffee he was thrown to the ground and hog-tied, then a handkerchief was shoved into his mouth so he couldn't scream. In this condition he was carried a few hundred yards down the river and thrown into a plum thicket. Then the boys got a shears and clipped the mane and tail of his fine Kentucky mare. Now letters were cut into the hair on her side, which read: "The Inspector is fixed," or words to that effect. Then the mare was turned loose and she ran towards home.

Now the herd was rounded up and put across the river, which had fallen during the night, so that there were only a few hundred yards to swim.

Soon a runner came to our camp and told the boss that the Wess Harding bunch of cowboys had got away with the Inspector, and that if he wanted to save the inspection fee—which would have amounted to two hundred and fifty dollars—and

the strays, he had better hurry across the river
before the mob came from Red River Station.

We lost no time in shoving the herd into the
river, thus saving the inspection fee, and a couple
of hundred strays, which were sold in Wichita,
Kansas, along with the balance of the herd.

While putting the herd across the river I did a
foolish thing, which has left a blotch on my con-
science to this day.

While the herd was being shoved into the water
by the yelling cowboys in the rear, I was stationed
between the high dirt bank and the waters edge, on
the right hand side, to keep the herd headed for
the other shore. The loud yelling of the cowboys
had brought a bunch of cattle out of the timber
on the run, with heads and tails up. They came
tearing towards me. There were about one hundred head, all fine blooded durhams.

I stood looking at these beauties with open-
mouth wonder until it was too late to run them
back. They went right into the herd and swam
across the river with the steers—thus adding gold
dollars to jingle in "Daddy" Grimes' pocket.
They were sold in Wichita, Kansas, for big
money.

The chances are some new settler further down
the river had brought this little herd from the
east, and, no doubt, much sleep had been lost hunting for them.

Nearly three years later in the fall of 1879, I

crossed Red River above Red River Station, and
made inquiry about the fate of the Inspector. I
learned that when his mare came home his wife
gave the alarm, and every male citizen in the village old enough to "tote" a gun started down the
river to search for the Inspector. He was found
in the plum ticket two days later; almost eaten
up by flies and mosquitos. And that after recovering he sold out his interests in Red River Station and returned to Kentucky.

In going through the Indian "Nation" we had
several bad rivers to swim. The Wachita, and the
South and North Canadians being the worst.

Large bands of mounted blanket Indians gave
us much trouble. They were in the habit of riding into camp when the cook was alone and eating
all the cooked grub in sight. They also demanded
the bosses to give them "who-haws", (steers) for
beef, or they would stampede the herd at night.
In this way these roaming bands from the Comanche, Kiowa, Kickapoo and Wichita Agencies, to
the westward, near the Wichita Mountains, kept
themselves well supplied with fresh meat. They
were the cause of many stampedes among the hundreds of herds passing up the trail at this season
of the year.

On reaching Salt Fork River our misery began.
After breakfast the boss had gone on ahead with
the two wagons. We had lately rigged up a
wagon to haul a supply of wood.

About ten a. m. the boss came running back and told us to hurry as fast as possible, as the river was rising fast. He said he managed to get the wagons over just in time, as the drift-wood and trees began flowing soon after.

When we arrived at the river she was about a half mile wide and full of drift-wood.

The lead steers were pointed into the foaming water. The boss and Otto Draub were on the left point, while Negro Gabe and I were on the right, to keep the leaders from turning back. Henry Coats was out in the lead, and the steers following him nicely.

When the water became deep enough to swim, Henry Coats' horse refused to swim. He fell over on his side, and in the excitement the lead steers turned back onto Gabe and me, and swam back to the shore.

We made a dozen efforts to get the herd back into the water, but failed. By this time it was raining, and the wind blowing a gale.

There we were in a fix, separated from our grub and bedding.

The wagons had gone on to the Pond Creek Stage Station, where now is located the prosperous town of Pond Creek, Oklahoma, a couple of miles from the river.

No doubt our failure to get the herd into the river was a God-send, for some of us might have been drowned. It makes it very dangerous for man and beast when struck by a swift flowing log or tree. Many trail boys have been drowned through this cause. Also horses and cattle.

Now we drove the herd down the river, a mile or two, where there was a belt of timber.

Late in the evening the rain ceased for a while, then a large camp fire was built of wet logs, and never allowed to go out during our stay here. Night and day the fire was kept burning. Being so large and hot the rain could't put it out. For supper a fat steer was butchered, and each cowboy not on duty with the cattle, roasted enough to satisfy his hunger. It had to be eaten without salt.

Early at night a new rain storm, with much lightning and thunder, broke out. Hence every man had to be in the saddle to stay with the drifting herd till daylight, by which time we were several miles from camp. Every now and then the whole herd would stampede.

Two days later Negro Gabe and I were hunting lost steers when we found an ear of yellow corn on the trail. That night we slipt off from the other boys and built a small fire to roast meat, and parch corn in the hot ashes. Gabe contended that God had dropped this ear of corn there for our special benefit.

The cold drizzling rain continued night and day. We managed to get a little sleep by rolling up in our saddle blankets, close to the camp fire.

Had it not been for the fact that the Cimarron and Wild Horse rivers were roaring torrents, other trail outfits would have arrived to furnish us with grub and bedding. We had the whole country between Salt Fork and Wild Horse to ourselves.

On the seventh day, in the afternoon, the boss, Hastings and I were hunting steers lost in a stampede the night before, when we saw the tents of a company of U. S. soldiers on the opposite side of Wild Horse, which was a roaring, swift flowing stream, about two hundred yards wide.

On being told by the captain that we could have all the grub we wanted by coming over to get it, I jumped my pony into the foaming water and swam across. Then a wash tub was borrowed from the captain's wife. This was filled full of flour, bacon, coffee, sugar and salt, and guided to the opposite shore. I swam by the side of the tub, landing several hundred yards below, being carried down by the swift current.

Now the tub was carried up stream and launched back into the water.

Thanking the captain's wife for the use of her boat, I mounted my pony and swam back to my companions.

A large tin can had been taken along to make coffee in, also a few small cans to be used as cups.

That night the boys had a picnic filling up. The

bread was baked by rolling it on sticks and holding it over hot coals.

The next morning the sun came out and there
was not a cloud in the sky.

This being the eighth day since separating ourselves from the mess-wagon.

The river had gone down so that we only had
about one hundred yards to swim.

The cook and driver of the wood wagon were
found well rested at the Pond Creek ranch.

Now we continued on "up the trail", passing
the noted grave of Hennessey, a cowboy killed
two years before, in 1874, by the wild Comanche
Indians, who had turned out on the war-path, killing every white person they came across.

Near his grave the town of Hennessey, Oklahoma, is now located.

At Bluff Creek, a few miles west of Caldwell,
we crossed over the line of the Indian "Nation"
and were in the Sunflower State.

On reaching the Ninnescah river, at the mouth
of Smoots creek, a permanent camp was established. Mr. W. B. Grimes, who had come around
by rail, was there to meet us.

When Mr. Grimes returned to Wichita, thirty
miles east, the boss and some of the boys accompanied him, to receive their summer's wages and
free railroad transportation back to Southern
Texas.

In those days it was the custom for all cowboys

who wished to return home, to receive free railroad tickets.

It was the fourth day of July when our camp
was pitched on the Ninnescah river.

The herd was split into three bunches to fatten
for the fall market. I remained with one herd of
800 steers. Our outfit consisted of a boss, four
cowboys, a cook and mess-wagon, with five saddle
ponies to the rider. Five miles east of the mouth
of Smoots Creek lived a New York family who
had taken up a quarter section of land and put in
a crop. From them we bought eggs and vege-
tables. They had acres of watermelons and canta-
loupes, but these didn't cost us a penny. All we
had to do was load the mess-wagon with dry cow-
chips from an old bed-ground and dump them at
the kitchen door, then load the wagon with melons.
These cow-chips being used as fuel, as there was
no timber or wood near by.

Soon after pitching camp on the Ninnescah, one
of our trail boys, John Marcum, entered a Government homestead in the forks of the Ninnescah
and Smoots Creek. He was laughed at as a "fool
hoeman," but he took the joking good-naturedly.

I have always had a desire to see this Marcum
farm, now that the country is thickly settled and
highly improved.

It was the first part of August before I had an
opportunity to see the cattle town of Wichita,
Kansas.

Another cowboy and I rode the thirty-five miles from camp in quick time. The first thing we did was to go to the New York store and fit out with new clothes from head to feet.

We found Wichita to be a livery town of about 2500 inhabitants. Now it is a city with eighty-five thousand population.

By the time the barbers got through fixing us up it was dark.

Now our ponies were mounted and we struck out in a gallop for Rowdy Joe's dance hall across the Arkansas river.. There were other dance halls across the river, but Rowdy Joe had the name throughout Southern Texas, of running the swiftest joint in Kansas—hence we steered for his place.

On nearing the toll bridge the one-legged man came out of his shanty to collect the twenty-five cents toll. We both went past him on the run, shooting our pistols off over his head. The poison liquor we had drunk since our arrival in town made us feel gay.

When half-way across the bridge the one-legged man turned both barrels of a shot-gun loose at us. We could hear the buckshot rolling along the bridge floor, under our ponies feet. One shot hit me in the calf of my left leg, and the scar remains to this day, as a reminder of Wichita's hurrah days.

It was in Wichita that Wild Bill made his rec-

ord as a killer of men, while acting as city marshall, and on one of the public streets Wess Harding a Texas man-killer, shot and killed one of his
own cowboys for wearing a stove-pipe hat. The
clerks in one of the stores had put it on his head
as a joke, and while walking down the street he
met Wess Harding, for whom he had come "up the
trail" with a herd of long-horns.

Wess Harding asked him to take that thing off
his head. He refused to do it, which cost him his
life, as West shot him dead. At least this was the
story told to the Rancho Grande cowboys by
"Shanghai" Pierce on his return from Wichita
that season.

The boys who returned with "Shanghai" Pierce
also told of how Wess Harding at Wichita, Kansas, beat "Shanghai" out of 300 fat steers.

In the late summer Wess Harding borrowed 300
fat steers from "Shanghai" to finish out a shipment that he was making to Missouri, promising
to replace the steers later, when the balance of his
herd became fat.

Late in the fall, when Mr. Pierce was closing
out his cattle interests at Wichita, to return home,
he wrote Wess Harding two or three "sassy" letters about the return of those steers. One day
they met at the Occidental Hotel. Wess put his
hand on his pistol saying: "Do you want those
steers now, Shang?" Mr. Pierce smelled blood in
the air, and in an excited manner, told Wess to let

the matter drop as he didn't need the steers. Thus
the debt was cancelled.

Late in the fall, after the first snow-fall a cowboy by the name of Collier and I concluded to go
to the Black Hills of Dakota, which was on a mining boom. Drawing our pay we rode into Wichita, I being mounted on a race pony, Whisky Pete,
which I had lately purchased.

In Wichita we "whooped her up Liza-Jane" for
a couple of days and nights and found ourselves
broke. Then we gave up the Black Hills trip and
started for the Medicine river, 100 miles west, to
hunt a winter's job.

In Kiowa Collier secured a job, while I drifted
down the river to where it empties into the Salt
Fork of the Arkansas. Here Maj. Drum had a
large cattle ranch and I figured on getting a job
there, but failed.

I met Maj. Drum, whose hair was then turning
white with old age, and strange to relate, he is still
living and has become a millionaire. He has offices in the Stock Exchange at Kansas City, Missouri, and looks after his money loaning business
with the vim of a young man. No doubt he is nearing the century mark.

I finally secured a month's job to help move the
Johnson herd of cattle down into the Indian "Nation".

We established the winter camp on the Eagle
Chief Creek, a tributary to the Cimarron River.

Before reaching there a severe snow storm and blizzard struck us, and I suffered greatly, standing night guard clad in summer clothes. The other boys had prepared themselves for winter. I didn't even have over-shoes or an over-coat.

Up to that time cattle had never been wintered in that part of the "Nation" on account of the danger from Indians. Mr. Johnson was called foolish for taking the risk.

After drawing my month's pay from the boss, Mr. Hudson, I spent a few weeks trapping, etc. I had built a dougout about a mile from the Johnson camp. One snowy day part of the Johnson herd drifted over the roof of my castle. One steer fell through, missing me by a foot. I came very near roasting before the blazing fire in the fireplace. Finally I got a chance to crawl under the steer's flanks and make my escape. Then I swore off trapping, leaving my pelts behind. I started for Kiowa, Kansas, next morning, and about three o'clock in the evening the raging blizzard became so cold I concluded to head for a warmer climate.

I had been facing the north wind. Now my course was turned to the southeast, down the Eagle Chief Creek.

After dark camp was pitched, but I went to sleep on my saddle blankets with an empty stomach, as I had brought no grub along, thinking I would reach the Drum ranch that night.

Now my route lay down the Cimarron river through sand hills and blackjack timber.

During the all-day ride many deer and turkey were seen, but I was afraid to shoot off my pistol for fear of attracting Indians—there being fresh moccasin tracks everywhere.

That evening a jack-rabbit was killed with a club when he hid in a bunch of tall grass. He went into my stomach for filling that night.

Early next morning while absent from my camp-fire to get a cup of snow from a drift a- gainst a high sand-hill, to be melted for drinking water, the tall grass around my camp caught fire. I had a swift job on my hands to save Whiskey Pete and my saddle. My Leather leggins and slick- er were burnt to a crisp. Only a small piece of sad- dle blanket was saved.

That night I had to sleep without even a saddle blanket to cover with, nor did I have fire to warm by, as my match box had burnt up with my slicker.

I hadn't gone far next morning when a fresh Indian camp, just vacated, was struck. After warming by the fire I continued down the river, knowing that I would soon strike the Chisholm cattle trail. It was struck during the evening, and I turned south on it. About five miles ahead of me was the band of Indians whose signs had been seen all along my route.

That night I camped with a government freight- ing outfit. They informed me that the fifty Kiowa

Indians who had just passed were returning to
their reservation from a hunting trip.

I slept with "Long Mike" that night, and next
morning he proved his Irish generosity by pre-
senting me with a pair of pants and a blue soldiers
overcoat.

The next evening I rode into Darlington—the
Cheyenne Indian Agency—on the North Canadian
River. Across the river stood Fort Reno, filled
with United State soldiers.

Since leaving Kiowa, Kansas, I had not seen a
house. Now, after more than forty years have
passed, you can imagine the number of fine houses that would be passed in going over the same
route. A "fool hoe-man's" dwelling now stands
on nearly every quarter section of land in that
part of Oklahoma.

After supper in Darlington, one of the clerks
in the store accompanied me a mile up the river
to an Indian camp, where they were having war
dances in preparation for their big medicine dance
soon to take place. It was a sight to me—half-
naked Indians covered with beads and feathers
cutting up all kinds of monkey-shines.

Every spring the Cheyennes held their big med-
icince doings up the river to test the grit of their
young bucks, who hoped some day to become "Big
chiefs."

Slits were cut thru the flesh of each side of the
breast. Now the would-be chief was hoisted upon

a tall pole. If he succeeded in tearing the flesh loose so as to fall to the ground he was considered "good medicine," and fit for a future chief. Otherwise he was branded as "bad medicine." Those who had the grit to tear themselves lose took great pride in showing the ragged scars as proof of their "good medicine". The Government finally put a stop to the cruelty.

After leaving the Cheyenne Agency I continued south on the Chisholm trail to the Wachita. Then my route was changed to the east, down that river.

I rode into Erin Springs—the home of a wealthy squaw-man by the name of Frank Murray—late one evening. The woods were full of Chicasaw Indians, and tough squaw-men, who had come to attend a big dance at Frank Murrays.

Whiskey was plentiful, being sold by Bill Anderson against the law. This Bill Anderson had served with Quantrell's band of confederate soldiers, and had since become an outlaw.

I joined the gay mob and danced with half-breed Indian maidens until daylight.

This I consider the wind-up of a foolish cowboy's first trip "up the Chisholm trail".

CHAPTER IV.

CAPTURING A BAND OF MEXICAN THIEVES.

A HERD OF BUFFALO LEAPS OVER MY HEAD. CHASED BY A WOUNDED BUFFALO BULL.

From Erin Springs I continued down the river to Pauls Valley—one of the richest spots on earth. Here it was no trick to raise from one hundred to one hundred and twenty-five bushels of corn to the acre, this corn sold for only ten cents a bushel. This brought many feeders to the valley to fatten steers for the market. Henry Childs and the Mitchells were the largest feeders in the valley.

Old Smith Paul, who was then ninety-two years of age, had been adopted by the Indians when a boy. When he grew to manhood he married an Indian girl and raised a brood of half-breeds. One of his sons was shot and killed years afterwards in Ardmore, Oklahoma, by his own son.

Smith Paul owned most of this large valley, as he had it under fence. According to the law and custom, any Chicasaw Indian, or squaw-man, held title to all the land that he was able to keep under fence—so that he didn't get nearer than a quarter of a mile of any one else's fence.

Most of this rich, black land he rented out to white farmers, who raised corn.

In the early spring of 1877, while I was in the valley, this husky old man married a sixteen year old Texas girl. I was told that they had three children before he died.

Here I spent the winter breaking wild ponies at two dollars and fifty cents a head. My home was with one of the renters on Mr. Paul's land.

While living with this renter and his splendid family I paid fifty dollars for one crack shot out of my new Smith & Wesson pistol. One of the boys and I were back of the house, and I was bragging of how I could knock a birds eye out every shot with this pistol. The boy pointed out a redbird sitting on a limb, in a clump of bushes saying: "Let me see you knock his eye out".

The eye went with the bird's head when I fired. The shot killed one of the renters fine work horses standing concealed further on. I was let off by paying fifty dollars, half the animal's value. During the winter a pretty little half-breed girl got me "plum locoed," and I came within an ace of marrying her. All that prevented was the fear that being a squaw-man might ruin my chance of becoming president of these glorious United States. My school books had taught me that every boy has an equal chance of becoming president.

In the late spring I drifted to Tishamingo, the capital of the Choctaw Nation—thence to Denison, Texas, and west to St. Joe, on the Chisholm trail.

Here, in May, I secured a job with one of the
north-bound herds of longhorns owned by Capt.
George Littlefield, of Austin, Texas.

This herd consisted of 3,500 head of mixed
cattle. One of Mr. George Littlefield's nephews,
Phelps White, now a millionaire stockman of Roswell, New Mexico, was one of the cowboys.

In Passing through the Indian "Nation" we
experienced many hardships in swimming swollen rivers. Dudley Pannell—later shot and killed
in Tascosa, Texas,—and I were the champion
swimmers of the outfit, and did most of the dangerous work in the water.

The herd being made up of mixed stock-cattle
it was a difficult matter to get them to take to the
water. Small bunches had to be cut off from the
main herd and shoved into the raging torrent.
Then naked cowboys would swim on each side of
the leaders to keep them headed towards the opposite shore.

Often when out in mid-stream the leaders would
turn around and go to milling in a circle. Once I
was caught in the center of the milling herd, and
to save myself from being jammed to death, I
crawled up onto the animals backs, working my
way from back to back until the edge of the herd
was reached.

Often these milling bands would drift with the
current a mile or two down the stream before we
could get them strung out again. To make them

string out we would swim near the edge and splash water in the nearest animals' faces, at the same time yell and "cuss".

When sure that the band would continue of their own accord, to the opposite shore, we would swim back after another bunch. Sometimes we would have to walk a mile or more up the river to the main herd, the swift current having taken us down the stream.

In order to get the mess-wagon over these raging streams, a log raft had to be made to float it over.

On crossing the Cimarron River, at the mouth of Turkey Creek, we switched off from the Chisholm trail and headed north-west for Dodge City, Kansas, via the U. S. Government Post of Camp Supply.

The reason for leaving the Chisholm trail was the fact that the "fool hoe-men" were fast settling up the grazing country west of Wichita.

We arrived in Dodge City, Kansas, on the third day of July. The herd was to continue on up to Ogallaly, Nebraska, and possible further north to Miles City Montana—both great cattle towns.

Therefore, I drew my pay and quit the job, to celebrate the glorious Fourth of July in the toughest cattle town on earth.

This celebration came near costing me my life in a freeforall fight in the Lone Star dance hall, in charge of the now noted Bat Masterson.

The hall was jammed full of free-and-easy girls, long-haired buffalo hunters and wild and wooly cowboys.

In the mix-up my cowboy chum, Wess Adams, was severely stabbed by a buffalo hunter. Adams had started the fight to show the long-haired buffalo hunters that they were not in the cowboy class. We had previously taken our ponies out of the livery stable and tied them near the hall. I had promised Adams to stay with him 'till Hades froze up solid.

The stab wound was in the back, under the shoulder blade.

After mounting our ponies, Joe Mason, a town marshal, tried to arrest us, but we ran him to cover in an alley, then went out of town yelling and shooting off our pistols.

By daylight we had ridden eighteen miles to the D. T. Beals' steer camp. Towards the last I had to hold Adams on his horse, he had become so weak from loss of blood. This wound laid him up for two weeks.

This incident illustrates what fools some young cowboys were after long drives ''up the Chisholm trail'', and after filling their hides full of the poison liquors manufactured to put red-shirted Irish rail-road builders to sleep, so that the toughs could ''roll'' them, and get their ''wads''. Instead of putting a cowboy to sleep it stirred up the devil

in his make-up, and made him a wide-awake
hyena.

At this time the Atchison, Topeka and Santa
Fe railroad was building west from Dodge City,
which filled the town full of cut-throats and bums,
who follow up new railroads.

The town was also the outfitting center for buffalo hunters within a radius of hundreds of miles,
and that year of 1877 she became the great long-
horn cattle center of the Universe, by Wichita
losing the trail drive through the "fool hoe-men"
settling up the cattle range to the westward.

The citizens of Dodge City seemed proud of
their fat grave yard in the 'Boot Hill' Cemetery,
where there were eighty-one graves, all the occupants having died with their boots on—in other
words killed, except one, who died a natural death.
A fine record for a town only one year old—that
is dating from the time she became a center for
cattle-men, buffalo hunters and railroad crews.

Fort Dodge, a government post, was located
only five miles distant, and the soldier boys added
merriment, as well as devilment to the little yearling city.

Other Kansas towns which attained distinction
as cattle shipping points, were Elsworth, Abilene,
Ellis, Great Bend, Hutchison, Nickerson, Newton,
Caldwell and Coolidge. The latter, being on the
western edge of the state, became a wild and wooly

town in the early '80s, when the "fool hoe-men" had settled up the country around Dodge City.

Abilene, Ellis and Caldwell took the lead in burying hilarious cowboys with their boots on.

Hunnewell, Garden City and Kingman won some distinction as cattle towns—and so did Medicine Lodge and Kiowa in later years.

The first long-horn cattle were driven north in the late '60s to Baxter Springs and Abilene, before Wichita became a town.

It was in Abilene that Joe McCoy shipped his first car-load of buffalos.

During the '70s Miles City, Montana, Cheyenne, Wyoming, Ogalally and Sidney, Nebraska, were wild and wooly cattle centers. From these places large herds were driven to the open ranges, where new ranches were established. Most of these new ranches began improving the long-horn cattle by introducing short-horn males.

One of these new ranches afterwards became noted as the Two-bar 70 ranch. It was located on Snake River, near Soda Springs, Idaho.

A wealthy citizen, by the name of Wm. E. Hawks, of Bennington, Vermont, established the ranch, and put his young son, Wm. E. Hawks, Jr., in charge.

Now, after the passing of over a quarter of a century, this man Wm. E. Hawks, Jr., has become the collector of the greatest store of cowboy literature and paraphenalia in the whole United

States. At his fine home in Bennington, Vt., he has what he proudly calls his "Two-bar 70 Tepee," where these relics are displayed.

In Bennington Mr. Hawks is known as the Historian of the Plains. He attracts much attention when riding his favorite cow-pony through the streets, wearing his cowboy sombrero, goat-skin leggins, etc.

Soon after the Fourth of July I secured a job with the David T. Beals outfit to drive a herd of young steers to the Pan-handle of Texas, where a new ranch was to be established.

Bill Allen, of Corpus Christi, Texas, was the boss, and Owl-head Johnson was the cook, and driver of the mess-wagon.

"Deacon" Bates one of Mr. Beal's partners, a dyed-in-the-wool Yankee, accompanied us for the purpose of selecting the new range.

After crossing the Cimarron River into No-mans-land—now a part of the State of Oklahoma—we saw our first herd of buffalos grazing a few miles to the southward.

Mr. Bates selected me to ride on ahead with him and get some fresh buffalo meat.

When within a mile of the herd, the ponies were tied in a gulch. Then we walked afoot out on the open flat, straight towards the wooly animals. When within about one hundred yards of them we raised our Sharps 45 caliber rifles and fired. Two young animals, a bull and a heifer, dropped over dead. Now the whole herd began bawling and milling around the fallen beasts.

I became frightened and wanted to run back to my pony, but Mr. Bates, who had ranched at Granada, Colorado, said buffalos were harmless unless wounded, when they became vicious.

Still I felt timid and allowed the "Deacon" to walk ahead.

On reaching the edge of the milling herd, he pulled off his hat and began shooing them out of his way. At first they seemed to pay no attention to him, but finally they started away on the run.

This trait of buffalo nature made it easy for hunters to slaughter them by the thousands. They will stampede at the sight of a horseman, but pay no attention to a man afoot.

A day or two later I roped my first buffalo. We had pitched camp for the night when a herd of the wooly animals ran past the camp, headed west.

I had just ridden out a few hundred yards to turn back some steers which were going into the sand hills.

At a break-neck pace I took after the fleeing buffalos, not realizing that my pistol and bowie-knife lay on the ground in camp, until after I had overtaken the rear end of the herd.

Now down came my lasso and an eight months old heifer was roped by the neck. The bawling of the calf brought the mother cow on the run. She made a dive for my pony. The thirty foot rope was tied hard and fast to my saddle horn, so that the rope couldn't be turned loose. By ''socking'' spurs to the pony I managed to drag the calf and keep out of the cows reach. She soon scampered off after the fleeing herd.

By this time I was many miles from camp, and it was getting dark.

I tried to throw the calf hard enough, so that she would lie still until I could reach her on foot. But the instant she struck the ground on her side she would be on her feet again.

Finally becoming angry I dismounted and went at her with all the strength in my make-up. She was soon hog-tied with my silk sash.

Now with a dull pocket knife I cut the throat and peeled her hide off. Then I tied a chunk of meat to my saddle and rode towards camp. It was now pitch dark.

After going east about a mile I concluded to ride south in hopes of finding a stream of water, as the pony and I were thirsty. The streams in that country all run from the west to the eastward—hence my hopes of finding water.

About three o'clock in the morning, while sound asleep on my saddle blankets, with the saddle for a pillow, a herd of stampeded buffalos came running by, a few hundred yards to the westward. The loud roar and the shaking of the ground frightened my mount and I was dragged quite a distance, the end of the hackamore rope having been wrapped around my body on lying down.

There I was left afoot on the prairie, and dying for a drink of water, but thanks to kind providence I soon heard a faint snort off to the eastward. The pony had stopped, and I was happy after mounting, and was headed towards the southeast. I knew by keeping this course we would strike the Bascom trail, over which the herd was being driven.

About ten, A. M. water was struck at the head of Sharps Creek, a tributary to the Beaver River, which was called the North Canadian further down stream.

About noon the cattle herd arrived on Sharps Creek, and camp was pitched. The outfit had traveled about fifteen miles from where I left them.

We had buffalo veal mixed with flour gravy for dinner. The boys complimented me on my skill as a meat rustler, with only a lasso as a weapon.

On arriving at the North Paladura Creek we saw the first house since leaving Crooked Creek, twenty-five miles south of Dodge City, this being a buffalo hunters trading store.

Now that country along the old Fort Bascom trail is thickly populated with ''fool hoe-men'', and towns have also sprung into existence, Diamond being one of them, with a population of three or four thousand.

When within fifty miles of the Canadian River, camp was established until "Deacon" Bates and I could locate a range large enough for 50,000 cattle.

We started early one morning with a pack horse loaded with grub and bedding.

On the north bank of the South Canadian River we landed in Tascosa, which contained half a dozen Mexican families, and a store owned by Howard and Rinehart. At this store liquor was also sold.

From here we rode down the river twenty-five miles, to the mouth of Pitcher Creek, where a Mr. Pitcher kept a buffalo-hunters trading-store. Across the river about 300 wild Apache Indians were camped, they being from Arizona on a buffalo hunt.

Now Mr. Bates and I put in a week riding down the river, nearly to Adobe Walls, where Tom Bugsby had established a cattle ranch the year previous, and south to the foot of the great Llano Estacado.   .

Finally Mr. Bates selected the site for the home ranch on a little creek about a mile east of Pitcher Creek. This to be the center of the future LX cattle range, which was to extend twenty miles up the river and the same distance down the stream, and twenty miles south to the

foot of the Llano Estacado (Staked Plains), also
twenty miles north to the foot of what was called
the North Staked Plans. This constituted a free
range forty miles square.

On our travels we had not seen a cow brute, and
the grass was fine. Although thousands of buffalo were roaming over this range, also deer and
antelopes by the hundreds. Hence we never ran
short of wild meat to eat.

Finally we returned to the herd and moved it
to the site of the home ranch, where the cattle
were turned loose to fatten on the fine buffalo-
grass.

Now Mr. Bates went to Granada, Colorado, to
over-see the moving of their thousands of well-
bred, shorthorn cattle to this new Panhandle
ranch.

Mr. David T. Beals and Erskine Clement—
one of Mr. Beals partners—were kept busy in
Dodge City, Kansas, buying long-horn steers to
put on this new range.

By the time snow began to fall this grassy LX
range contained thousands upon thousands of
cattle.

Above Tascosa a Mr. Goodrich had a small cattle ranch, and down the river twenty-five to fifty
miles Tom Bugsby and Hank Creswell controll-
ed the range. South of us there was not a cow-
brute until reaching the Paladuro Canyon (head
of Red River), a distance of about fifty miles,

where Cattle King Charlie Goodnight, had established a large cattle ranch the year previous.

Mr. Goodnight had the pick of the whole country when his ranch was selected. Nature had fenced his range down in the Paladuro Canyon. The valley down in the canyon being from one to five miles wide and about thirty miles in length, with walls on each side hundreds of feet high. There was only one place in the canyon where cattle could climb out, and a few rods of stone fencing fixed this. At the head of the canyon there was an abrupt wall. At its mouth Mr. Goodnight established his home ranch.

In the early winter Mr. Phelps White arrived with a herd of long-horns and established the L I T ranch above Tascosa. These cattle, and others which came later, were owned by Mr. White's uncle, Capt. Geo. Littlefield, the wealthy banker of Austin, Texas.

During the winter Lee & Reynolds established the L S ranch near Tascosa. Also Jim Kennedy— a son of the cattle king, of southern Texas— brought in a herd of steers and turned them loose above Tascosa.

In the late fall Nick Chaffin—now a respected citizen of Las Vegas, New Mexico—established the Pollard ranch on lower Blue Creek, at the northeast edge of the LX range.

Early in the winter I started out alone down the Canadian River in search of some lost steers. I

stopped at Adobe Walls to view the ruins of that
noted place, where, in 1874, fourteen buffalo hunters—the notorious Bat Masterson being one of
them—stood off a large band of Comanche Indians, killing hundreds of them with their long-
range buffalo guns, for several days, until the
United States soldiers arrived. Skulls and bones
of dead Indians still lay on the ground near this
old stockade.

On this trip I had the pleasure of meeting Mr.
and Mrs. Thomas Bugsby at their home ranch
near Adobe Walls. I was told the history of their
courtship, which sounds like a dime novel story.

In the fall of 1876 Mr. Bugsby was driving
through Kansas with a small herd of fine blooded
short-horn cattle, in search of a free range.

In pitching camp one day, near a farm house,
he discovered that they had lost their axe.   He
walked to the farm house to borrow one. The
farmers young daughter brought him the axe, and
at the same time, from her bright eyes, shot his
system full of Cupid's little arrows.

The next morning when Mr. Bugsby returned
the axe, he proposed marriage to this handsome
young lady, and after papa and mamma were
consulted, the deal was made.

A Justice of the Peace tied the knot, and then
the journey to the wild Panhandle of Texas was
continued, with a new girl cook to dish up the
grub.

A year or so later a girl baby was born—the only white child in that part of the country. She was called the "white papoose" by the Indians. But when about eight years old, she—an only child—met a horrible death from the bite of a mad skunk.

Further down the river I stopped at the Cresswell cattle ranch, and formed the acquaintance of Cattle King Hank Cresswell, and his foreman, Tom McGee, the afterwards sheriff who was murdered by express robbers at Higgins, Texas.

From there I rode to Ft. Elliot, a Government Post, where the noted man-killer, Clay Allison, had just proved his bravery.

At the Suttler's Store he was making things uncomfortable for some of the officers and clerks. He was on one of his periodical drunks, and no one could do anything with him. Finally the commanding officer was sent for to have Clay put out of the store.

This commanding officer was swollen to the bursting point with West Point dignity. Walking up to Clay he pointed a pistol in his face and demanded that he leave the store at once, and never return.

Allison looked him in the face and called him all the hard names imaginable. He told him that he was a coward, and didn't have the nerve to shoot. Then he gave him one minute to put up his gun or he would fill him full of lead.

The officer put up his gun and walked out of the store, pale and trembling, at least this was the story told to me.

Clay Allison had already killed eighteen men, some of them at Cimarron, New Mexico.

At a restaurant in Cimarron he sat down at the same table with a bitter enemy by the name of "Chunk." When the waiter called for his order he said: "Give us hot coffee and pistols for two." This meant war, and "Chunk" drew his pistol, but too late, as Clay had put in the first shot, which was fatal.

In later years a dentist in Pueblo, Colorado learned that Clay Allison was a dangerous man to monkey with—although he didn't know it in time.

Allison had an aching tooth and stepped into the dentist's office to have it pulled. Seating himself in the chair the dentist began fumbling with what he supposed was the aching tooth, as it had a large cavity. Shoving the dentist's hand aside Clay told him that he was fooling with the wrong tooth.

This angered the dentist and he told him to keep quiet—that he knew his business, and didn't need any advice. "Alright," answered Clay, "If you know your business go ahead, but don't you pull the wrong tooth."

The molar was jerked out, but the aching one continued to do business.

Now Clay struck Mr. dentist across the head

with his heavy Colts pistol, which "floored" him.
Then getting the forceps he pulled every tooth
out of the front part of this tooth-doctor's upper
jaw. The Colorado papers came out with the account of it later.

At this time Clay Allison had a small cattle
ranch on Gagsby Creek, a tributary of the Wachita River.

From Ft. Elliot I rode down Sweet-water Creek,
five miles, to the "wild-and-wooly" town of
Sweet-water. Here there were two large outfitting
stores, run by McCamy and a Mr. Weed, also several saloons and dance-halls. She was a lively
place at night when the cowboys and buffalo-
hunters turned themselves loose.

During my two days stay in Sweetwater I became chummy with a saloon proprietor, who
showed me the fine, silver plated, ivory-handled
Colts, 45 caliber pistol, willed to him a short time
previous by the noted horse-thief, "Chubby"
Jones. The story of "Chubby" Jones' death, was
also told to me by this saloon keeper, and others
in the town. I was already familiar with the history of "Chubby" Jones and his boss, "Dutch
Henry," whose right name was Henry Born. All
cowboys in the Indian "Nation," and the Texas
Panhandle, knew of these two noted characters.

It was claimed that "Dutch Henry" was at the
head of 300 horse-thieves who operated between
Venita, Indian Territory, and Pueblo, Colorado.

The bands who stole horses in the "Nation" would meet a band with stolen horses from Colorado, at some point in No Mans Land, and swap herds—the Colorado thieves returning to that state, and the others back to "The Nation."

The undoing of "Chubby" Jones, as told to me, happened as follows:

A company of soldiers from Ft. Elliot rounded up "Chubby" and eight of his gang, on lower Sweetwater Creek. In the fight the army captain was shot through the stomach. This angered the soldiers who hung the nine thieves to a tree that night.

When they started to string up "Chubby" Jones he asked, as a last request that his pistol be given to the above saloon keeper, which request was promised and carried out.

Later I saw a newspaper account of "Dutch Henry" being in jail at Pueblo, Colorado, for stealing ten Government mules. Many years later he settled down as a respectable citizen of Summitville, Colorado, where he still resides, according to my latest information.

The hanging of "Chubby" Jones, and his eight followers, and the capture of "Dutch Henry," broke up the worst gang of horse-thieves in the west.

About the summer of 1878 the town of Sweetwater died a natural death. The town of Mobeta, near Ft. Elliot, sprang into existance and killed Sweetwater.

Now the county of Wheeler was organized, and Mobeta became the county-seat—with jurisdiction over all the un-organized counties to the westward, to the New Mexico line.

A ride of 80 miles brought me back to the LX ranch with a small bunch of lost steers.

I found a new boss in charge of the ranch, Mr. Allen having returned to his home in Corpus Christi, and an outlaw by the name of Wm. C. Moore had taken his place.

This man Moore, up to a short time previous, had been the manager of the large Swan Cattle Company, of Cheyenne, Wyoming. He had just shot and killed his negro coachman, and made his get-away from the law officers in Wyoming, landing at the LX ranch on a broken down pony. Previous to this he had shot and killed his brother-in-law in the state of California, which brought him to Cheyenne, Wyoming, to begin life anew.

Bill Moore was a natural leader of men, and one of the best cow-men in the west. He could get more work out of a gang of cowboys than any man I ever knew. But while working so hard for the LX outfit he was feathering nis own nest by stealing from them. He soon started a brand of his own, and established a ranch at Coldwater Springs, in No Mans Land. He had two of the LX cowboys in with him on these steals, and they tried to induce me to join them, but I refused, as it was against my principle to steal from my employers.

A few years later Moore sold his ranch and cattle for $70,000. Then he quit the LX outfit, and with this money established a cattle ranch in the American Valley, of western New Mexico. His stay in the American Valley was short, as he shot and killed two men, which placed a large reward on his head.

Many years later, as a detective, peddling whiskey among the Chilcat and Chieke Indians in the wilds of Alaska, I met Bill Moore going under an assumed name. At that time I was a detective running down two thieves who had stolen $10,000 worth of gold from the great Treadwell, Alaska, Mining Company.

On this trip I was mounted on the hurricane deck of a 40 foot Indian canoe, painted with all the colors of the rainbow. The gold was recovered, and the two thieves sent to the penitentiary.

After returning from Ft. Elliot a young Texan by the name of John Roberson and I were put in a camp on the head of Amarillo Creek, at the foot of the Llano Estacado, about fifteen miles south of the home ranch. Our duty was to prevent cattle from drifting onto the Staked Plains. The cattle were in the habit of following bands of buffalo south, onto the plains, and we experienced much hardship in cutting them off from the running buffalo herds. The cattle couldn't run fast enough to keep up with the wooly beasts, but they would stay on their trail until turned back.

The company furnished us with free ammunition to shoot into these roving bands of buffalos, in order to keep them off the range. .

Soon after locating our camp on Amarillo Creek the main herd of buffalos migrating from the north, passed a mile west of us. For three days and nights there was a solid string of them from a quarter to a half mile wide—sometimes in a walk and at other times on the run.

During daylight we could look to the northward, across the Canadian River breaks, a distance of about thirty miles, and see this black streak of living flesh coming down off the north plains. Their route was down Pitcher creek, a mile west of our home ranch.

The next morning after this great string of wooly animals had crossed the Canadian River breaks, I trailed a bunch of cattle south onto the plains. It was an easy matter to distinguish the cattle tracks from those made by buffalos. The former are sharp pointed while the latter are round pointed.

The cattle were found with the buffalo at Amarillo Lake—where the thriving little city of Amarillo, Texas, is now located.

I found the whole Llano Estacado one solid black mass of buffalo—just as far as the eye could reach, to the eastward, southward and westward.

The great herd had scattered out to graze on the thickly matted buffalo-grass, nearly a foot high. There must have been a million of the wooly beasts.

Shortly after this Mr. Moore had me accompany him to the head of Paladura Canyon, so as to learn the country.

Here I saw my first expert lancing of buffalo, by Apache Indians on swift buffalo horses. I accompanied a band of these reds out to a grazing herd, about 50,000 in number.

When within a mile of the herd the Indian chief lined us all up abreast—that is side by side—close together. This being done to fool the buffalo—as they would have stampeded at the sight of horse-men.

They paid no attention to us until we were within a few hundred yards of them. Then they began to bunch up. Now we made a charge as fast as the horses could run. This started a stampede, and the lancing began at the rear end of the herd.

Steel and stone lances were attached to long poles. The lance was driven into a buffalos loin, and down he would go, helpless, but not killed.

Some of the Indians on the swiftest horses were almost in the center of the herd, lancing one buffalo after another as they ran.

I did nothing but watch them at their expert work. Just ahead of me a buck on a yellow horse reached over to the right to bury the sharp lance into a buffalos loin when his weight on the slender wooden handle, about fourteen feet long, snapped it in two, and down went Mr. "Ingin" rolling in the grass. Buffalos were dodging all around him. When he sprang to his feet a cow jumped over his head and knocked him down. Then he sat still until the rear end of the heard had passed. While sitting there some of the beasts jumped over him.

At the wind-up of this free show I shot a buffalo and tied his hump-loins to my saddle for supper.

For a mile or two back, the plain was covered with hundreds of buffalos trying to rise to their feet. Soon the hundreds of old bucks, squaws and children arrived and butchered these struggling animals for their hides and meat.

About Christmas we had an exciting chase after thieves. Moore had sent a runner from the home ranch after Roberson and me to help round up 8 Mexicans who had robbed Mr. Pitcher of everything he had. They had loaded all of his store goods into large freight wagons and headed across the plains in a southwesterly direction.

We, nine of us, rode night and day until they were overtaken near the line of New Mexico.

For a while they stood us off with their long-range buffalo guns.

Finally Moore sent Jack Ryan to their barricaded wagons, under a flag of truce. They agreed

to haul the stuff back and turn it over to Mr.
Pitcher, who was one of the pursuing party, on
our promise not to harm them.

This was agreed to, and we all started back towards Pitcher Creek. It had been promised that
they could retain their fire-arms, but while camped for dinner we got the drop on them and took
away their arms.

Now it was proposed to hang them all to a big
cottonwood tree in the head of the gulch, where
we were camped.   But Dudley Pannel and I
protested that this would be cowardly after giving
our words of honor that they would not be harm-
ed.

As Pannel and I were well thought of, Mr.
Moore decided in our favor, and several lives were
saved.

Now Roberson and I returned to our camp at
the foot of the South Plains.

One morning I found cattle tracks among those
of a large band of buffalos. I went on their trail
in a gallop on my blue pony. The trail continued
up onto the plains past Amarillo Lake.

A ride of about twenty miles brought me in
sight of the buffalo herd, about 50,000 in number.
On reaching within a mile of them they stampeded
towards the southwest. Now my misery began,
trying to separate the dozen or more cattle from
them.

It was almost night when my mount gave completely out and could hardly trot. Then I turned back towards camp, in a slow walk, for a night ride.

Just as the sun was getting ready to go to roost I saw a band of Indians coming towards me from the west, on the run. Their steel lances were glistening in the sun.

I thought of running, as they might be on the war-path, but despite the spurring, my mount couldn't be made to gallup.

Now my Winchester rifle and Colts 45 caliber pistol were examined to see if they were in trim for war.

When they galloped up to me I was standing facing them, with the rifle raised for action. The leader passed the time of day in the Mexican tongue, which I understood. Then he made inquiry as to whether I had seen any buffalo. Of course I told him about the herd which I had just left.

Seeing that my mount was played out this Apache chief invited me to go with them to their camp, a few miles west. The invitation was accepted, as I was hungrier than a wolf.

After filling up in this Indian camp I went to sleep in a tepee, filled with squaws and papooses.

By the latter part of January the buffalo had all gone south, with the exception of a few straggling bands. One of these bands, about one hundred head, made me think of the hereafter on the other side of the great divide, where Saint Peter lives.

Being out of meat, and seeing this band grazing at the head of a gulch, about a mile distant, I concluded to get some buffalo humps.

In order to make sure of fresh meat I kept out of sight, by riding in the bed of the gulch.

When within a few hundred yards of the grazing band the pony was left with the bridle-reins hanging on the ground, to prevent him running away.

Continuing the journey up the arroyo afoot, I came to the extreme head of it, a steep embankment. Now standing on my tip-toes a grassy valley spread out before my eyes, and over its surface grazed the contented animals, all but one old bull, lying down chewing the cud of contentment, within twenty or thirty feet of my nose.

This being the only animal within sure gun-shot I concluded to make a death shot on him. Then the rifle barrel was raised gently up onto the level ground. But I was not tall enough, even by standing on my tip-toes, to keep the rifle butt pressed to my shoulder, and at the same time bring the sight down on the sleeping bull. Hence the rifle was fired off-hand like a pistol.

Aim was taken under the hump, where the bullet strikes the lights, and causes death.

At the crack of the gun the bull was on his feet and jumping towards me. Ducking my head down he leaped over me and fell dying in the bed of the gulch, at my feet. I sweated blood through fear that he might regain his feet and discover me.

Now peeping over the edge of the embankment I discovered the whole band almost upon me. I squatted down and they leaped over my head onto the dying and struggling bull. In looking upward all I could see was flying buffalos. The dirt bank caved in around me, through some of the animals getting too near the edge before making the leap for the bottom of the arroyo.

I felt relieved when the last ones went over me, and went running down the gulch.

No doubt this old bull was their leader, and seeing him, at the crack of the gun, go over this embankment they followed.

After getting the loose dirt out of my clothes, the hump-loins were cut out of the dead bull, and a start made for camp. My pony had stampeded on seeing the narrow gulch filled with wooly beasts running towards him. He was found trembling with fright about a quarter of a mile from where I had left him.

Soon after this I had a different kind of buffalo experience.

Seeing a lone bull grazing on a flat I rode to a round knoll, which hid me from his view. When within about one hundred yards of the small hill I left the pinto pony, with the bridle-reins hanging on the ground. Then crawling to the top of the knoll I fired a bullet from my Winchester rifle at the bull. He dropped to the ground, and I foolishly stood up.

In an instant the bull jumped to his feet with one front leg as limber as a rag. The bullet had hit him in the shoulder.

He saw me while standing in plain view, a distance of about one hundred and fifty yards. Here he came for me with his front leg dangling at his side. The broken leg seemed to have no effect upon his speed.

Instead of pumping more lead into him, as the lamented "Teddy" Roosevelt would have done, I started for my mount on the run. The rifle went up in the air when I started. It was a case of my legs running away with me.

Once I looked back. That was enough, the bull was coming down the knoll not fifty yards behind me. My hair raising on end threw my sombrero off my head.

My greatest fear was that "Pinto" would become frightened and ran before I could leap into the saddle. But he stood still until I could make the leap—then he wheeled around and was off like a bullet, just in time to save my bacon. The bull's horns raked some of the hide off his rump before he could get out of reach. As I sprang into the saddle the bridle-reins wer' grabbed with my left hand.

Now I rode around to my rifle and Mr. Bull was killed, and his hump-loins taken to camp.

That night "Pinto" received a double feed of corn for saving my life.

CHAPTER V.

A TRIP TO CHICAGO AS COW-PUNCHER.

MY FIRST ACQUAINTANCE WITH OUTLAW "BILLY THE KID."

Towards spring Mr. Moore put a cowboy in my place, to camp with Roberson, and I was sent out with a scouting outfit to drift over the South Staked Plains in search of stray cattle. Our outfit consisted of a cook, Owl-head Johnson, and three riders, Jack Ryan, Van Duzen and myself. After starting on this trip we experienced a touch of hardship. Camp was pitched after dark one evening on the edge of a "dry" lake, or basin. Enough buffalo-chips were gathered to cook supper.

After retiring under our tarpaulins, spread over the beds on the ground, a severe snowstorm sprang up. By daylight our beds were covered with a foot of snow.

Crawling out of these warm beds into the deep snow made it anything but pleasant. We had no buffalo-chips to build a fire—hence had to cut up the bed of the mess-wagon.

There we were afoot on these snowy plains, as
the pony staked out the evening before had pulled
up the stake-pin and drifted south with the hobbled ponies. They were not found until late that
evening, about ten miles from camp.

It was on this trip that I saw the piles of bones
from thousands of ponies killed by orders from
General McKinzie. They were at the head of
Tule Canyon, which empties into Canyon Pali-
duro.

It was here that General McKinzie and his
United States soldiers rounded up the 7,000 Comanche Indians, in 1874, when they broke away
from Ft. Sill, Indian Territory, on the war-path—
killing hundreds of white men.

The Indian ponies were shot and killed to prevent another break on horse-back, the reds being
made to walk back to Ft. Sill.

One forenoon 3,000 Comanche Indians gave us a
"scaring up," as we didn't know whether they
were on the war-path or not. On Mulberry Creek
they came pouring down the hills from the eastward, on a gallop. We were completely surrounded.

The chief made inquiry about buffalos to the
westward. They were from Ft. Sill, Indian Territory, on a big buffalo hunt. The chief showed us
a letter from the commanding officer at Ft. Sill
stating that they were peaceable, and friendly toward the white men.

Before reaching Ft. Elliot we ran into thousands of Cheyenne and Pawnee Indians on hunting trips.

After an absence of several weeks we arrived back at the LX ranch with a small bunch of steers.

About the last of March all the cowboys were called in from the outside line-camps to prepare for the spring round-up.

Mr. Moore hired every renegade outlaw and cowboy passing through the country for this big spring round-up.

One evening before bed-time the sky became red from a big prairie fire off to the south-eastward.

The fire was being driven by a strong southeast wind, down into the Canadian River Breaks, from the Staked Plains.

Now the headquarter ranch became a busy place. Saddle ponies were rounded up and a start made for the big fire, by the dozens of cowboys.

In a swift gallop Moore led the crowd in the pitchy darkness, over all kinds of rough places.

A ride of about fifteen miles brought us to the fire. Then we became fire-fighters in dead earnest.

Large droves of cattle were running ahead of the fire. Some of these largest animals were shot and killed.

Then the carcasses were split open. Now two cowboys would fasten their ropes to each hind leg

of the dead animal, and by the saddle-horn drag
it to the blaze.

If the fire was down in an arroya, where the
blue-stem grass grows tall, it was allowed to burn
its way onto a level flat covered with short buffalo
grass. Here the two cowboys dragging a carcass
would straddle the blaze—the one on the burnt
side close up, with his rope shortened, while the
other, on the hot smoky side, would be at the extreme end of his rope.

Now the wet carcass was dragged slowly along
the blaze. This would put out the fire, all but small
spots. These being whipped out by cowboys following afoot with wet saddle blankets, or pieces of
fresh cow-hide.

A few miles of dragging in a hot blaze would
wear a carcass into a frazzle. Then another animal was killed to take its place.

Without a bite to eat, except broiled beef without salt, this strenuous work was kept up until
about three o'clock the following evening, when
the fire was under control, and our range saved.

We arrived back at the ranch about sun-down—
a smoky, dirty, tired and hungry crowd.

Soon after this fire excitement Mr. Moore lost
nearly half of his crew of cowboys. They "hit the
trail for tall timber," in New Mexico and Arizona—some on stolen ponies.

The cause of this cowboy outlaw stampede was
the arrival of E. W. Parker—now a respected

citizen of El Paso, Texas—and his large, well
armed crew of Government Star-route mail sur-
veyors. But they kept their mission a secret,
hence the boys had them spotted as Texas Rangers in disguise.

A few months later the first mail route in the
Panhandle of Texas was established. It ran from
Ft. Elliot, Texas, to Las Vegas, New Mexico, a
distance of about three hundred miles. Our home
ranch was made Wheeler post-office.

Previous to this all our mail came from Ft.
Bascom, New Mexico, two hundred and twenty-
five miles west, on the upper Canadian River. It
came by private conveyance, and each letter sent,
or received, cost us twenty-five cents—news-
papers the same.

By the middle of April our range was crowded
with buffalo again. They were migrating north.
But there was no great herd like the one going
south in the early winter.

Not over half of the wooly beasts which went
south ever returned. They had been slaughtered
for their hides, worth one dollar each, at the south
edge of the Llano Estacado. It was estimated
that, during the winter, there were 7,000 buffalo
hunters along the Texas Pacific Railway—then
building west to El Paso.

Now these buffalo were going north through
Kansas and Nebraska to their summer feeding

ground in Dakota, to be killed by the northern hunters.

The following fall only a few scattering herds passed through the Canadian River Breaks, on their way south. Most of these met their doom that winter by the southern hunters. Thus were the millions of buffalo wiped from the face of the earth in a few years.

About the middle of April Moore took all his cowboys, about twenty-five with two well filled mess-wagons, and went to Tascosa, there to meet other outfits from different parts of the country. Many of these cattle outfits came from the Arkansas River in southeastern Colorado, and southwestern Kansas.

When we pulled out of Tascosa for the upper Canadian River, there were dozens of mess-wagons, and hundreds of riders.

This gerenal round-up, the first ever pulled off in the Texas Panhandle, started work near Ft. Bascom, New Mexico, and continued down the river almost to the Indian Territory line.

During the winter thousands of northern cattle had drifted south and lodged in the Canadian River Breaks. These were all driven north after the general round-up.

While these round-up crews were at Tascosa, that little burg saw the need of saloons and dance-halls to relieve the wild and wooly cowboy of his loose change. For the supply of liquors, sardines

and crackers in Howard & Reinhart's store melted
away like a snow-ball would if dropped into
Hades.

In June, after the spring round-ups, our cattle
were all shoved onto the summer range, on Blue
Creek, north of the river.

I and another cowboy were placed at the extreme head of the Blue, to ride line. Our camp
was pitched at a spring.

Every morning and evening I had to ride
past a plum-thicket, which was a few miles west
of our camp, at the edge of which lay the bodies
of three murdered Mexican buffalo hunters. They
were badly swollen, and the sight of them made
me nervous.

Strange to relate these corpses were never de-
voured by the many lobos and coyotes around
them. This fact convinces me that there is truth
in the theory that wolves won't eat a dead Mexican—possibly on account of his system being im-
pregnated with chilli, (red peppers).

A short time previous, these three men were
murdered by Nelson and three companions, in order to get their ox-teams to haul buffalo hides to
Dodge City, Kansas.

These murderers were never arrested, as there
was no law in the country—and not a law-officer
nearer than Ft. Elliot.

While camped at the head of the Blue, several

herds of "Jingle-bob" cattle passed near our camp.

These thousands of cattle had belonged to cattle king John Chisum, of the Pecos River, in New Mexico, until Colonel Hunter, of the firm of Hunter and Evans in southern Kansas, had played a "Dirty Irish" trick on him.

In the early '70s John Chisum had bought thousands of she cattle from the old battle-scarred Confederate soldiers in middle Texas, giving his notes as pay.

These cattle were driven across the Staked Plains to the Horse-head crossing of the Pecos river—thence up the river over two hundred miles into New Mexico, where they were turned loose.

Then Mr. Chisum introduced fine-blooded short-horn bulls to breed out the long horns on these Texas cattle.

The notes given by Chisum for these cattle were finally outlawed, as they couldn't be collected in New Mexico.

In the winter of 1877 and '78 Col. Hunter and his flowing grey beard hiked from Medicine Lodge, Kansas, to middle Texas and bought up these outlawed notes for five and ten cents on the dollar.

These notes were tucked into a satchel, and in the early spring of '78 taken to Las Vegas, New Mexico, and placed in a bank.

Now Col. Hunter went overland down the Pecos

to South Spring River, where Mr. Chisum had established his ''Jingle-bob'' headquarter ranch.

There a deal was made for about 20,000 head of his picked cattle, at a fancy price.

Now Jesse Evans, Col. Hunter's partner, went to Dodge City, Kansas, and hired fifty fighting cowboys to go to New Mexico after these cattle.

As soon as the Chisum outfit got a herd ''put up'' they were turned over to the Hunter and Evans cowboys.

When the last herd was gathered, and headed north-eastward, for the line of Texas, Col. Hunter and John Chisum went overland to Las Vegas to settle up.

Among cattle-men Col. Hunter's word was as good as his bond, hence Mr. Chisum had no fear about getting his pay.

The curtain of this ''dirty Irish'' play goes down when, in the bank, the old satchel was opened and Mr. Chisum was paid for the cattle in his own notes, with the years of accumulated interest.

As fast as a team could travel, John Chisum went back to his ranch. Then he tried to make up a fighting crowd to follow up these Hunter and Evans herds, and recover them. He offered ''Billy the Kid'' and his warriors big inducements to do the job, but they knew the Hunter and Evans cowboys were armed to the teeth, and being already over the line in Texas, they declined.

In the middle of June Mr. Moore sent for me

to take charge of a herd of steers containing 2500 head. I was told to take them out onto the south Staken Plains and fatten them. My crew consisted of four riders, and a cook to drive the mess-wagon, with five ponies to the man.

Soon after this three more herds of steers were sent to the South Plains and I was put in charge of the four herds. This made me feel of some importance. I had nothing to do but ride from one camp to the other—sometimes twenty miles apart —to see that the steers were kept on fresh range so as to put on fat by the time cold weather set in.

The summer of 1878 was a wet one—hence the "dry" lakes, or basins, were full of rain water.

During the summer Mr. David T. Beals paid me a visit. He brought a young man, Burkley Howe, from Massachusetts, and turned him over to me to be taught the cow-business.

The first lesson I dished out to Burkley Howe was on mustang meat.

I shot and killed a young mustang from a band of 300 head. Then a young buffalo was killed. Some of the meat from each animal was taken to camp. I instructed the cook to prepare each kind the same, but to have it in separate vessels.

When we squatted down on the grass to eat our supper, the cook pointed out the vessel containing the mustang meat, which in reality was the buffalo meat. Of course the other boys had been posted.

Burkley Howe could not be induced to even taste the horse meat. Instead he filled up on the supposed buffalo beef, which he declared was the finest he had ever eaten. When told of the trick, after supper, he was mad all over, and tried to vomit. This goes to show that the mind controls the taste.

About the first of October 800 fat steers were cut out of my four herds and started for Dodge City, Kansas.

The balance of the steers being turned loose on the winter range, along the Canadian river.

Now I secured permission from Mr. Moore to overtake the fat steer herd and accompany them to Chicago.

Mounted on my own pony, Whiskey-Pete, I started in company with a cowboy named John Farris. We kept on the Bascom trail.

After crossing the Cimarron river we saw a band of about two hundred Indians, off to our left, in a deep arroyo, traveling westward, single file. Being hungry we concluded to gallop over to them and get something to eat.

On seeing us coming they all bunched up and showed great excitement. This didn't look good to Ferris and me, so we galloped back to the Bascom trail and continued north.

About sundown we reached Mead City, a new town started a few months previous. Here there were a half dozen new frame buildings, their insides being turned "topsy turvy," showing that the Indians had run the occupants off and ransacked the dwellings. There were Indian moccasin tracks everywhere.

Now we hurried on to the store, on Crooked Creek, arrived there after dark. Here we found the same conditions as at Mead City, showing that the Indians had looted the store. Hearing some ox-bells down the creek we rode to them, about a mile distant. Here we found several yoke of oxen and a log cabin, the door of which was locked.

Being hungry the lock on the door was broken, and we entered. A playful puppy inside gave us a hearty welcome.

After the lamps were lighted we found sacks of grain for our tired ponies, and a cupboard full of nice food.

Hanging over the still warm ashes in the fireplace was a pot of fresh beef stew. This proved a treat, and we filled up to the bursting point.

About midnight we started on the last lap of our 225 mile journey.

A twenty-five mile ride brought us to the toughest town on earth, Dodge City.

It was now daylight, and the first man met on the main street was Cape Willingham, who at this writing is a prosperous cattle broker in El Paso, Texas.

Cape gave us our first news of the great Indian

outbreak. He told of the many murders committed by the reds south of Dodge City the day previous—one man being killed at Mead City, and another near the Crooked Creek store.

Riding up the main street Ferris and I saw twenty-five mounted cowboys, holding rifles in their hands, and facing one of the half dozen saloons, adjoining each other, on that side of the street.

In passing this armed crowd one of them recognized me. Calling me by name he said: "Fall in line quick, h—l is going to pop in a few minutes".

We jerked our Winchester rifles from the scabbards and fell in line, like most any other fool cow- boys would have done.

In a moment Clay Allison, the man-killer, came out of one of the saloons holding a pistol in his hand. With him was Mr. McNulty, owner of the large Panhandle "Turkey-track" cattle outfit.

Clay, who was about half drunk, remarked to the boys in line that none of the S——b's were in that saloon."

Then a search was made in the next saloon. He was hunting for some of the town policemen, or the city marshall, so as to wipe them off the face of the earth. His twenty-five cowboy friends had promised to help him clean up Dodge City.

After all the saloons had been searched Mr. Mc-

Nulty succeeded in getting Clay to bed at the Bob Wright Hotel. Then we all dispersed.

Soon after, the city law-officers began to crawl out of their hiding places, and appear on the streets.

Clay Allison had sworn to kill the first officer found—and no doubt he would have done so.

I found Mr. Erskine Clement, a partner of Mr. Beals, at the Wright Hotel, greatly worried over the non-arrival of the steer herd, which Mr. Moore had written him had started two weeks previous. He was surprised when told that I had seen no sign of them having come over the Bascom trail.

Telegrams kept pouring in from the west, of the bloody deeds committed by the Indians, on their way to Dakota. They were Northern Cheyennes, who had broken away from the Cheyenne Agency in the Indian Territory.

That evening at the Wright Hotel I heard a captain from Ft. Dodge, five miles east of Dodge City, say that he would round up this tribe of reds or leave his dead body on the ground. He and his company of soldiers were waiting for a west bound train. A week later he was killed in a battle which took place.

In passing through western Nebraska these Indians murdered many settlers. At one ranch-house they captured a widow woman and her two daughters. After a days march they turned the mother loose on the prairie, stark naked, keeping her two daughters with them.

After much hardship this woman found the cabin of a "fool hoe-man," who was living alone. He wrapped the robe of Charity and his overcoat around her, and took her to civilization.

About midnight my chum, John Ferris, was flat broke, and borrowed twenty-five dollars of my accumulated wages, amounting to over $300. He had in this short time "blowed in" his $114.00. By morning he had borrowed $50.00 from the livery man on his pony and saddle, and I had to get these out of "soak" for him, before he could hit the road again.

He went direct to Ft. Sumner, New Mexico, where he was shot and killed by Barney Mason, one of "Billy the Kid's" gang, and a brother-in-law of the fearless New Mexico sheriff, Pat Garrett.

The next morning after my arrival in Dodge City, Erskine Clement and I struck south to look up the lost herd of steers.

We found the outfit traveling up Crooked Creek very slowly. They had quit the Bascom trail to avoid long drives between watering places. This, no doubt, had saved them from running into the Indians.

In Dodge City the herd was split in two, 400 head being put aboard of a train for Chicago. I went in charge of this first shipment, and Mr. Clement followed with the next.

Two of the cowboys went with me, one of them being A. M. Melvin, who now, after forty years, lives with a happy family at No. 11, Blackinton Street, Orient Heights, East Boston, Mass.

Now for the first time in my life I became a cow-puncher, carrying a lantern and a long pole with a spike in the end, to keep the steers punched up, when they got down in the crowded cars.

In a few years the name, Cow-puncher, became attached to all cowboys.

At Burlington, Iowa, we crossed the Mississippi River into Illinois, and there on the east bank of the great river unloaded to feed the steers.

During our two days stay we three cow-punchers made a dozen or more trips on the ferry boat to Burlington, a swift city. Our trips were free, and everything in the way of liquor, cigars, meals, candy, etc. bought in Burlington were free.

The fact of us wearing our cowboy outfits, including chaparejos, pistol and spurs may have had something to do with the people refusing to take money from us. But is was said that their object was to encourage cattle-men to ship by way of Burlington.

On the first night after leaving Burlington I came within an ace of being ground to death by the train. The thoughts of my narrow escape cause my flesh to creep, even to this day.

A sleet storm was raging. The train stopped to take on coal. We three cow punchers left the caboose and ran up towards the engine, peeping through the cracks to see if any of the steers were down.

About the time we reached the engine the train started. Then we climbed onto the first car and started back to the caboose, on the run. I was in the rear. In making a spring from the top of one car to the other—the space between being about two feet—my high-heel boots slipped on the icy boards. There I lay flat on my back with my head and shoulders over the open space. I had grabbed the edge of the footplank with my right hand. This is all that saved me from sliding down between the cars.

Mr. Beals met us on our arrival in Chicago. After unloading at the stock yards he took me to dine with him at the Palmer House. He wanted me to take a room in his hotel, but I told him that the food and price, five to ten dollars a day, were too rich for my blood. Therefore I went to the Irvine House where the price was only $2.00 a day.

That night I turned myself loose in the toughest part of the city, spending all the money I had, about $200.00.

Towards daylight I managed to find my way back to the Irvine House, where a nap was taken.

About ten a. m. I struck out for the Palmer

House to borrow some money from Mr. Beals. On the way there, while gazing up at the signs, I saw the name of Dr. Bruer, Dentist. This put me in mind of the teeth which needed filling, so up the stairs I went, not realizing that my pockets were empty of cash.

In the dentist office I found Mr. Bruer and his handsome young lady assistant.

After seating myself in the dentist chair, the doctor asked me what kind of filling I wanted for the two teeth. I told him to fill them with gold.

In those days the filling had to be done by hand. The doctor used the punch and the young lady the mallet. They didn't stop for lunch. It was three p. m. when the job was finished.

Now I got down off the chair, and for the first time realized that I didn't have a cent to pay for the work.

I asked the amount of my bill, and was told that it was $45.00. I told the doctor that I would drop around in the morning and pay him. He turned pale, and so did his assistant. The large pistol and bowie-knife buckled around my waist may have caused them to turn pale.

Finally the doctor asked the name of my hotel. I told him. Then he said: "Now you wont forget to come up in the morning and pay me?" I answered him that he could depend upon it.

I found Mr. David T. Beals at the Palmer House and borrowed $100.00. Then I started out to see more of the sights of a great city. But I took the precaution to tuck the dentist's $45.00 down in the watch pocket of my pants, so that it wouldn't be spent.

The next morning at nine o'clock I was in the dentist's office and paid over the $45.00. The doctor and his assistant were happily surprised.

The doctor had me go to lunch with him. Then we spent the afternoon driving over the city in his buggy, drawn by a fine pair of black horses.

We visited the water-works and climbed up to the top of the tall, round tower, from the inside. On reaching the top I looked over the edge, to the ground below, just once. That was enough. I was afraid the thing would topple over from my weight. The dentist laughed at me, but he couldn't induce me to look over the edge again.

After the drive was over I hunted up Mr. Beals to get more money for the night's sight-seeing.

I can look back now and see that I was an "easy mark" for the city people. Of course they knew at a glance by my bowlegs and high-heel boots where I was from, and they charged be according-ly, for what was purchased.

After a few days sight-seeing I boarded a train for Dodge City, Kansas. Mr. Beals and Erskine Clement accompanied me.

Shortly after leaving Chicago I became very angry towards my employer, for not giving a poor blind beggar some loose change.

This old blind man had passed through our car leaving each passenger a slip of poetry, to be returned if a donation was not given.

When the old man returned through the car gathering up his little sheets of poetry, I waited to se how much money Millionaire Beals would give him. Not a cent did he give. This caused me to boil over with rage, although nothing was said. Reaching my hand in my pants pocket all the loose change therein was grabbed and handed to the poor blind beggar. It amounted to two or three dollars.

After the blind man had passed on, Mr. Beals said: "You are foolish Charlie to throw your money away. That old cuss is rich. You ask the conductor when he comes through about him." I did so, and the conductor told me that this blind beggar lived in one of the swell residences of Chicago, and was considered wealthy. This caused my anger to flop from Mr. Beals to my own fool self.

On our way west Mr. Beals "harked back" to his early life, telling me of how he struggled at a shoe-makers bench, in Massachusetts, to accumulate his first $500.00.

With this sum in his pocket he drifted to Deadwood, Dakota.

In a mining camp, across a range of mountains from Deadwood, he opened a boot and shoe store, ordering his stock of goods on credit, from his home town in the east.

After one year in business, his profits footed up $60.00. The next year it amounted to $60,000, partly in gold dust. He then sold out the business and walked with two hired men, carrying the gold dust, to Salt Lake City, Utah, there taking a stage-coach for Denver, Colorado, where he located, building the first iron-front store building ever put up in Denver.

Arriving in Dodge City, Whiskey-Pete was mounted early one morning for my 225 mile lonely ride to the LX ranch.

I arrived at the headquarter ranch late in the evening.

A crowd of strangers were playing cards under a cottonwood tree near by. The cook informed me that they were "Billy the Kid" and his Lincoln County, New Mexico, warriors.

When the cook rang the supper bell these strangers ran for the long table. After being introduced, I found myself seated by the side of good-natured "Billy the Kid". Henry Brown, Fred Waite and Tom O'Phalliard are the only names of this outlaw gang that I can recall.

When supper was over I produced a box of fine Havana cigars, brought from Chicago as a treat for the boys on the ranch. They were passed around. Then one was stuck into my new $10 meerschaum cigar holder, and I began to puff smoke towards the ceiling.

Now "Billy the Kid" asked for a trial of my

cigar-holder. This was granted. He liked it so
well that he begged me to present it to him, which
I did. In return he presented me with a finely
bound novel which he had just finished reading. In
it he wrote his autograph, giving the date that it
was presented to me.

During the next few weeks "Billy the Kid" and
I became quite chummy.   •

After selling out the band of ponies, which he
and his gang had stolen from the Seven River
warriors, in New Mexico, he left the Canadian
river country, and I never saw him again.

Two of his gang, Henry Brown, and Fred
Waite—a half-breed Chicasaw Indian—quit the
outfit and headed for the Indian Territory.

During his long stay around the LX ranch, and
Tascosa, "Billy the Kid" made one portly old
capitalist from Boston, Mass., sweat blood for a
few minutes.

Mr. Torey owned a large cattle ranch above
Tascosa. On arriving from the east he learned
that "Billy the Kid" and gang had made themselves at home on his ranch, for a few days—
hence he gave the foreman orders not to feed
them, if they should make another visit. This order reached the "Kid's" ears.

While in Tascosa "Billy the Kid" saw old man
Torey ride up to the hitching rack in front of
Jack Ryan's saloon. He went out to meet him, and

asked if he had ordered his foreman not to feed them.

Mr. Torey replied, yes, that he didn't want to give his ranch a bad name by harboring outlaws.

Then the "Kid" jerked his Colts pistol and jabbed the old man several times in his portly stomach, at the same time telling him to say his prayers, as he was going to pump him full of lead.

With tears in his voice Mr. Torey promised to countermand the order. Then war was declared off.

Thus did Mr. Torey, a former sea captain, get his eye-teeth cut in the ways of the wild and wooly west.

This story was told to me by "Billy the Kid," and Steve Arnold, who was an eye witness to the affair. But the "Kid" said he had no intention of shooting Mr. Torey—that he just wanted to teach him a lesson.

CHAPTER VI.
AN ELEVEN HUNDRED MILE HORSEBACK RIDE DOWN THE CHISHOLM TRAIL.
I BOSS A HERD OF STEERS "UP THE TRAIL" FROM THE GULF COAST OF TEXAS.

After laying around the home ranch a few weeks Mr. Moore put me in charge of a scouting outfit, to drift over the South Staked Plains, in

search of any cattle which might have escaped
from the line-riders.

While on this trip I went to church several
times.

A colony of Illinois Christians, under the leadership of the Reverend Mr. Cahart, had established the town of Clarendon, on the head of Salt
Fork, a tributary of Red River, and there built a
white church house among buffalo and wolves.

Clarendon is still on the map, being the county
seat of Donnely county, Texas.

When spring came I was called in from the
plains and put in charge of a round-up crew, consisting of a cook and twelve riders.

Our first round-up was on the Goodnight range,
at the mouth of Mulberry Creek. Here we had the
pleasure of a genuine cattle-queen's presence.
Mrs. Goodnight, a noble little woman, a dyed in
the wool Texan, whose maiden name was Dyer,
attended these roundups with her husband.

Mrs. Goodnight touched a soft spot in my heart
by filling me up on several occasions, with juicy
berries which she had gathered with her own
hands.

At this writing Mr. and Mrs. Charlie Goodnight
are still alive, and living in the town of Goodnight,
Texas, which has been made famous as the home
of the largest herd of buffalo in that state, and
possibly the whole United States.

The foundation of this herd of buffalo was started on this round-up in the spring of 1879.

In the round-up at the head of Mulberry Creek was a lone buffalo bull. When ready to turn the round-up cattle loose Mr. Buffalo was roped and thrown, and a cow-bell fastened to his neck. When turned loose he stampeded, and so did the thousands of cattle.

. In the round-up the following spring the bell-buffalo was with the cattle, and had with him several female buffalos.

During that summer Mr. Goodnight fenced his summer range on Mulberry Creek, and this small herd of buffalo found themselves enclosed with a strong barbed wire fence.

From what I was told Charlie Goodnight increased this buffalo herd by having cowboys rope young animals to be put inside the Mulberry Creek fenced pasture.

Many years afterwards I rode through this tame herd of buffalos, near the town of Goodnight.

We wound up this spring round-up on the Rocking Chair range, at the mouth of McClellan Creek, where I saw about 50,000 cattle in one bunch— more than I had ever seen before in one band.

Now we returned to the home ranch with about 500 LX cattle, which had drifted away from the range during the winter.

Shortly after our return Mr. Moore had us help

him brand some large long-horn steers, late arrivals from South Texas.

We did the branding on the open plains, at Amarillo Lake.

While roping and tying down these wild steers we had great sport in seeing "Center-fire" saddles jerked over sideways from the pony's back, the riders with them.

Mr. Moore had got his cowboy training in California, where they use "center-fire", high horn saddles, and riatas, (ropes) which they wrap around the saddle-horn when roping on horseback. The cinchas on these saddles being broad, and in the center of the saddle, which makes it difficult to keep the saddle tight on the pony's back

Mr. Moore had persuaded many of his cowboys to use these saddles and the long rawhide "riatas"—hence a large order had been sent to California in the early spring. In the order were many silver mounted spurs and Spanish bridle bits. I sent for one of these ten dollar bridle bits, and am still using it to ride with.

I must confess that Moore never got a fall from his "center-fire" saddle, as he had learned his lesson early in life. He was also an expert roper with his 75-foot "riata." He could throw the large loop further and catch his animal oftener than any man in the crowd of about twenty-five riders.

Moore tried his best to persuade me, and such

Texas raised cowboys as Jim East, Steve Arnold and Lee Hall, not to tie our 30-foot ropes hard and fast to the saddle horns when roping large steers. He argued that it was too dangerous. No doubt he was right, but we had been trained that way.

Later poor Lee Hall was gored to death by a wild steer, roped down in the Indian Territory. The steer had jerked his mount over backward, and one of his spurs caught in the flank cinch, preventing him from freeing himself until too late to save his life.

The spur which hung in the cinch and caused his death, was one of the fine silver mounted pair which Moore sent to California for.

After his death I fell heir to Lee Hall's spurs and they are used by me to this day, over 40 years later.

In the latter part of June Mr. Moore put me in charge of 800 fat steers for the Chicago market. My outfit consisted of a well filled mess-wagon, a cook and five riders.

We headed for Nickerson, Kansas, on the Arkansas River, across country through No-Mans-Land—now the 30 mile strip of Oklahoma which butts up against New Mexico on the west, and on the north is bordered by Kansas and Colorado, the Texas Panhandle being the south border.

Late in the fall we arrived in Nickerson,

Kansas, and turned the steers over to "Deacon" Bates.

Leaving Whiskey-Pete and a Missouri mare, which I had traded for, with a "fool hoe-man," five miles south of town, "Jingle-bob" Joe Hargraves and I started west across country to meet another herd of fat steers.

As the snow had begun to fly it was thought best to turn this herd towards Dodge City, Kansas—hence we being sent to pilot the outfit to Dodge City.

While on this lonely ride I came within an ace of "passing in my checks." We ran out of grub and for supper one night filled up on canned peaches, without anything else to eat with them. All night these juicy peaches held a war-dance in the pit of my stomach, and before daylight I was all in. "Jingle-bob" Joe wanted me to pray, but I told him that I would wait a little longer, in hopes that I might pull through.

Joe Hargraves was not much on the pray himself, but I believe he has a passport to heaven for one kindly act done the winter previous. He was on his way to Dodge City, over the Bascom trail, when he stopped for the night on the Cimarron River, where a short time previous a small store had been established.

The next morning a "fool hoe-man" and his hungry and ragged family drove up in a covered

wagon drawn by two skinny ponies. They were
half starved and didn't have a cent of money.

"Jingle-bob" Joe asked the store man what he
would take for all the goods in his place. He set
the price at $150.00, which was accepted. Then
the goods were loaded into the "hoeman's" wagon, and he drove off singing "Home, Sweet
Home". He was looking for a free home to settle
on.

We finally found the steer outfit and turned
them towards Dodge City. There the fat steers
were put aboard two trains, and I took charge of
one train, thus taking my second lesson in cow-
punching, with a spiked pole and lantern.

As on the former trip the steers were unloaded
across the Mississippi River from Burlington,
Iowa, and fed.

In the city of Burlington we punchers were
treated royally. None of the candy and ice-cream
merchants would take a penny from us. Everything in that line was free.

On arriving in Chicago Mr. Beals met us. Then
at the Palmer House Mr. Beals settled up my
wage and expense account. With a few hundred
dollars in my pocket I started out to see the
sights again.

I had told Mr. Beals of my intention to quit his
outfit and spend the winter in Southern Texas.
He agreed that if I concluded to go back to work
for the LX company in the spring, he would ar-

range for me to boss a herd of steers up the trail. Said he had already contracted with Charlie Word of Goliad, Texas, for two herds to be delivered on the LX Ranch.

A couple of days and nights sight-seeing put me almost "on the bum", financially. Then a train was boarded for Nickerson, Kansas.

Whiskey-Pete and the bay mare were found hog fat. The "fool hoe-man" had shoved corn to them with a scoop shovel.

After purchasing a pack-saddle, and some grub, I had just six dollars in cash left to make my eleven hundred mile journey down the Chisholm trail to the gulf coast of Texas.

Puck was not far off when he wrote: "What fools these mortals be." For here was a fool cowboy starting out to ride eleven hundred miles, just to be in the saddle, and to get a pony back home.

On the way down the trail I kept myself supplied with cash by swapping saddles, pack pony, watches, and running races with Whiskey-Pete, who was hard to beat in a three hundred yard race.

At one place in middle Texas I laid over a couple of days to rest my ponies, and to make a few dollars picking cotton.

One morning I was sent out by the farmer, with a bunch of bare-footed girls, to pick cotton in a field which had already been picked over.

These young damsels gave me the "horse-laugh" for my awkwardness in picking the snowy balls of cotton.

When night came I had earned just thirty cents, while the girls had made more than a dollar each. This was my last stunt as a cotton picker.

On Pecan Creek, near Denton, I put up one night at the home of old man Murphy—the father of Jim Murphy, who was a member of the Sam Bass gang of train robbers, and whose name is mentioned in the Sam Bass song, which was a favorite with trail cowboys.

The old Chisholm trail was lined with negroes, headed for Topeka and Emporia, Kansas, to get a free farm and a span of mules from the state government.

Over my pack there was a large buffalo robe, and on my saddle hung a fine silver-mounted Winchester rifle. These attracted the attention of those green cotton-field negroes, who wore me out asking questions about them.

Some of these negroes were afoot, while others drove donkeys and oxen. The shiny black children and half-starved dogs were plentiful. Many of the outfits turned back when I told them of the cold blizzards and deep snow in Kansas.

My eleven hundred mile journey ended at the old Rancho Grande headquarter ranch, after being on the trail one month and twelve days.

The balance of the winter was spent on hunting

trips after deer and wild hogs, and visiting friends throughout the county of Matagorda.

Early in the spring I mounted Gotch, a pony traded for, and bidding Whiskey-Pete goodbye, he being left with my chum, Horace Yeamans, we headed for Goliad to meet Charlie Word. He was found near Beeville, thirty miles west of Goliad, putting up a herd of long-horn steers for the LX company. He had received a letter from Mr. David T. Beals telling him to put me in charge of one of the herds.

This first herd was to be bossed "up the trail" by Liash Stevens.

The outfit was up to their ankles in sticky mud, in a large round corral, putting the road-brand on the steers, when I found them. I pitched in and helped, and was soon covered with mud from head to feet. Each steer had to be roped and thrown afoot, which made it a disagreeable job in the cold drizzling rain. And to finish out the days work, after my thirty mile ride from Goliad, I stood guard over the steers until after midnight.

Mr. Word had just purchased a band of "wet" ponies from old Mexico, and I showed my skill in riding some of the wildest ones.

One large iron-grey gelding, which the Mexicans said was a man-killer, broke my cinchas and dumped me and the saddle into the mud. Then he pawed the saddle with his front feet until it was ruined. I had to buy a new saddle to finish breaking this man-killing broncho. But he proved to be a dandy cow pony when tamed.

After the herd had been road-branded and turned over to Mr. Stevens and his crew of trail cowboys, Charlie Word asked me to help him get the herd started on the trail.

Our first night out proved a strenuous one. Mr. Stevens had taken a fool notion to arm his cowboys with bulls-eye lanterns, so that they could see the location of each other on dark nights. He had ordered a few extra ones and insisted on me trying one that night, which I did.

About ten o'clock a severe storm came up and we were all in the saddle ready for a stampede.

While I was running at break-neck speed, to reach the lead of the herd, my pony went head over heels over a rail fence. The light from the lantern had blinded him, so that he failed to see it in time.

The pony was caught and mounted, and the new-fangled bulls-eye lantern was left on the ground.

Strange to relate, this lantern is prized today as a souvenir of bygone days. It was picked up next day by a young rancher, who, at this writing lives near Kingston, Sierra County, New Mexico.

I finally reached the lead of the herd, and from that time 'till daylight it was one stampede after another.

Daylight found young Glass and me alone with about half the herd of 3700 head. We were jammed into the foot of a lane, down which the cattle had drifted during the last hour of darkness.

This lane was built with five strands of new barbed wire, and was cut off by a cross fence. Here the herd was jammed together so tightly that it was impossible to ride to the rear.

There we had to wait and pray that another ʾtampede wouldn't start while hemmed in on three sides by a high wire fence. A stampede would have, no doubt, sent us to the happy hunting ground.

It required two days hard work to gather up steers lost during the night. They had become mixed up with range cattle.

In that camp the price of bulls-eye lanterns took a tumble. It was almost impossible to give one away.

After the herd was strung out again on the trail I went to Goliad to meet Charlie Word.

Here he made up a crew of twelve riders, a cook and mess-wagon, with five ponies to the rider, and turned them over to me. With this crew I drifted northwesterly to the crooked-street, straggling town of San Antonio,—now one of the leading cities of Texas.

In San Antonio we had all of our ponies shod, as we were going into a rocky country.

When out of San Antonio about fifty miles a bucking broncho "busted" a blood vessel in my bread basket. Being in great misery, and unable to sit up straight in the saddle, I concluded to ride back to the Alamo City and consult that great German doctor, Herff. The crew were instructed to lay over until my return.

In San Antonio I made inquiry as to where Doctor Herff could be found.

Riding up to a large, old-fashioned, stone residence I found this noted doctor—more than ninety years of age—hoeing in his garden. He informed me that he had turned his practice over to his son.

I found Dr. Herff, Jr. living in a fine two-story stone mansion. He laid me on a couch and examined the seat of pain. He pronounced a blood vessel stretched out of shape, so that the blood was not flowing through it—hence the great pain.

He told me to go back to camp, and on rising every morning, for a couple of weeks, to drink all the water I could possibly hold, and then, immediately afterwards, to drink that much more. He said this was all the medicine I needed. His charge was fifty cents for the examination and advice.

The next morning after reaching camp I took a half-gallon coffee-pot down to the creek and filling it drank it empty. It seemed impossible to drink any more, but by a great effort the coffee pot was emptied again.

After the first morning it was no trick at all to drink a gallon of water at one sitting.

In a few days I was completely cured, and the

memory of Doctor Herff and his half-dollar fee
will stay with me to the grave.

Now we continued the journey up the Llano
River.

On reaching Kimble County we laid over in a
new village called Junction City, now the prosperous seat of government of Kimble county, to lead
up our mess-wagon with grub, etc.

Further up the river we came to the end of our
journey, at the Joe, and Creed Taylor ranches.
We established camp on Paint Creek, in a very
rough, rocky country.

Charlie Word had bought 2500 head of cattle
from Joe Taylor, and it was our duty to gather
them from this range.

Mr. Creed Taylor had raised a son, "Buck"
who was a reckless, daredevil. He was buried with
his boots on—that is, shot and killed.

In the beginning of the '70s, around Quero, in
Victoria County, Texas, a bloody feud raged between the Taylor and Sutton gangs.

In one of their bloody battles in the town of
Quero, it was reported that nine men were killed.

About thirty-five years later I tried to obtain
the truth of this report.

In the little city of Las Cruces, New Mexico,
lives one of these noted feudists. He is a highly
respected banker and cattle raiser. It is said that
he lay in jail, on account of the Taylor-Sutton

fued, seven long years before being freed by the higher courts.

About the year 1914 I happened to be in Las Cruces, and concluded to find out the truth about this bloody battle in Quero.

I was stopping at the Park Hotel, owned by the president of the First National Bank of that town. This gentleman had been brought up in the neighborhood of Quero, and believed the story was correct, about nine men being killed in one battle, when the Taylor and Sutton gangs met. This didn't satify me, so I told the gentleman that I was going to visit this noted feudist at his bank and find out the truth.

He advised me not to do it, as it would result in me being kicked out of the bank, if I mentioned the subject.

On walking into the feudist's bank, he met me with out-stretched hand, and conducted me to his private desk in the rear.

I introduced myself as an early day Texas cowboy who had worked for ''Shanghai'' Pierce. He knew ''Shanghai'' well, and had much to say in his favor.

After we had talked about different subjects, I finally said: ''Oh, by the way, is it true that there were nine men killed in Quero one night when the Taylor and Sutton crowds met?''

In all my long life I never saw a man change so suddenly from a smiling, good-natured man to a scowling demon. His black eyes shot sparks of fire and he straigntened up in his chair, striking the desk with his fist, saying: "You bet it is true, we killed them knee-deep that night!"

Just then three men came into the bank and told him to hurry up, as they were waiting for him.

Here he begged my pardon for having to leave me, but he said he had to go out in the country to look at some cattle.

When he uttered the above expression I felt relieved, for it seemed that he was getting ready to kick me out of the bank.

I met the gentleman many times afterwards, but never alone, so as to renew the subject.

About the same time that the Taylor-Sutton feud was raging, there was another bloody feud being enacted in Jackson and Colorado counties, between the Stafford and Townsend gangs. "Tuck" Townsend was the leader on one side and Bob Stafford on the other.

Bob Stafford was a wealthy cattle owner, of Columbus, on the Colorado river.

Only a few of Bob Stafford's warmest friends knew the secret of how he became crippled in the left hand. It happened thus:

Stafford was riding along the road on a skittish horse. On the ground near by sat a twelve year old German boy eating his noonday lunch.

Near by grazed his small band of sheep, which he was herding.

The boy's dog ran out and scared Mr. Stafford's mount. Then he drew his pistol and killed the dog.

Now the boy sprang to his feet, and pulling his powder and ball pistol, opened fire on Stafford, who at once began shooting at the boy. But his horse jumping around made his aim untrue.

Bob Stafford had emptied his pistol, while the boy had only shot twice, and was taking aim for the third shot.

Here Stafford threw up his right hand, which held the pistol, saying: "Don't shoot, I'm empty."

The boy replied: "Alright, load up." Then he squatted down on the ground, and taking his powder horn from his shoulder proceeded to load the two empty chambers of his six-shooter.

Stafford replied, as he rode away: "No, I've got enough!" He was wounded in the left hand from one of the boy's shots.

Later Mr. Stafford rewarded the boy for his cool bravery.

Now, on the Creed and Joe Taylor range, we began gathering 2500 head of wild cattle. It was the hardest job of my life, working from daylight 'till dark, and then standing night-guard half the night.

As a rule bosses don't stand guard at night, excepting when there is danger of a stampede. But in order to keep my crew in a good humor I took my regular turn. The boys were worn out, and were almost on the eve of striking, from having to work twenty-six hours out of every twenty-four, as they expressed it.

Finally we got the herd "broke in," and started "up the trail," but not "up the Chisholm trail," which lay to the eastward about 100 miles.

During that spring of 1880 the Chisholm trail was impassible for large herds, as "fool hoe-men" had squatted all over it, and were turning its hard packed surface into ribbons with plows.

When about fifty miles west of Ft. Worth, Charlie Word, who had come around by rail, drove out in a buggy to see how we were getting along, and to supply me with more expense money.

At Doan's store, on Red River, we found Liash Stevens waiting for us. We swapped herds, as it had been decided to drive the herd I was with up into Wyoming.

I arrived at the LX ranch with 3700 head of steers on the first day of July.

Now part of my crew were paid off, and with the balance, six riders, I took the herd onto the South Staked Plains to fatten the steers.

Shortly afterwards I rode into Tascosa, and saw the great changes which had taken place since my last visit, a year previous.

Now there were three saloons and two dance-halls running full blast. Also the foundation laid for a new Court House.

The county of Oldham, with Tascosa as the County-seat, had been organized, and twelve unorganized counties attached to Oldham County.

My cowboy friend, Cape Willingham, had been appointed sheriff of these thirteen counties.

One of the first things I did after riding into Tascosa was to step into Mr. Turner's restaurant to see his pretty daughter, Miss Victoria Turner. I was not hungry, but to have the pleasure of this pretty miss waiting on me I was ordering all the good things in the restaurant. Just then a gang of cowboys came charging through the main street shooting off pistols.

As this was no uncommon thing for a live cow-town, I didn't even get up from the table.

In a moment Sheriff Willingham came running into the cafe with a double-barrel shot-gun in his hand. He asked me to help him arrest some drunken cow-boys who had just dismounted and gone into Jack Ryan's saloon, near by.

Just as we reached the Ryan saloon these cow-boys came out. One of them sprang onto his horse, when the sheriff told him to throw up his hands. Instead of throwing up his hands he drew his pistol. Then Willingham planted a charge of buck-shot in his heart, and he tumbled to the ground dead.

The dead cowboy was the one the sheriff was af-

ter, as he had seen him empty his pistol at a flock
of ducks, which a lady was feeding out of her hand,
as she sat in a door-way.

In galloping down the street this cowboy remarked to his companions: "Watch me kill some
of those ducks." He killed them alright, and the
woman fainted.

These nine cowboys had just arrived "up the
trail" with a herd of long-horn cattle, and were
headed for the north. For fear they might make a
raid on him that night, which they threatened to
do, the sheriff had me stay with him till morning.

Thus did Tascosa bury her first man with his
boots on, which gave her the reputation of being
a genuine cow-town.

From now on Tascosa's "Boot-hill" cemetery
began to show new-made graves. The largest killing in one night being six. At that time my cowboy friend, James H. East, now a well-to-do citizen of Douglas, Arizona, was sheriff. He held the
office for four terms, and helped to lay many wild
and wooly cowboys under the sod, with their
boots on.

Before the court house and jail were finished
Tascosa had a bad murder case to try. The District Judge, and attorney, came from Mobeta to
try the case.

Jack Ryan was foreman of the jury, and the
upstairs part of his saloon was selected as the
jury room.

When the prisoner's case was finished the jury were locked up over the saloon.

About midnight Jack Ryan and some of the jury men were holding out for murder in the first degree.

About that time Frank James, Ryan's gambling partner, got a ladder and climbed up to the outside window of the jury-room. He then called for Ryan, and told him that there was a big poker game going on in the saloon, and that he needed $300.00.

Jack gave him the money from the bank-roll, which he carried in his pocket, at the same time telling him to keep the game going until he could get down there, and take a hand.

Now Ryan called the jury men together and told them about the big poker game down in the saloon. He said it was necessary for him to be there and help Frank James out—hence he had come to the conclusion that the prisoner was innocent, and had no evil intentions of murdering his victim.

In a few moments Ryan had the few stubborn jury-men on his side, and the prisoner was declared innocent. At least this is the story told to me by men who claimed to know the facts of the case. This added another laurel to Tascosa's brow as a wide-open cow-town.

The following year Tascosa put on city airs by the arrival of a young lawyer by the name of Lu-

cius Dills, who hung out a shingle as Attorney at
Law.

During that fall the first election of Oldham
County was held and Mr. Dills was elected the
first County Judge. He was appointed District
Attorney for the whole Panhandle district, com-
prising twenty-four counties, before his term as
judge expired. Then he tore down his shingle as
Attorney at Law, and moved to Mobeta, thus Tascosa lost her first lawyer.

In the spring of 1885 Mr. Lucius Dills quit the
Panhandle country and moved to Lincoln County,
New Mexico, finally settling down in Roswell as
editor of the Roswell Record. Here he married the
lovely daughter of Judge Frank Lea, Miss Ger-
trude, and at the present writing has two pretty
daughters. He is now Surveyor General for the
State of New Mexico, and lives in Santa Fe,
where his friends are counted by the hundreds.

CHAPTER VII.

"BILLY THE KID'S" CAPTURE.

I ESCAPED ASSASSINATION BY A SCRATCH.

About the first of September my steer herd was
turned loose on the winter range. Then we started
out to brand calves.

When the branding season was over Moore sent me onto the South Plains in charge of a scouting crew.

A month later a runner hunted me up to deliver a letter from Moore. In this letter I was instructed to turn the outfit over to James McClaugherty, and to bring three of my picked fighting cowboys with me to the headquarter ranch.

I selected James H. East, Lee Hall and Cal Polk as the fighting men.

On arriving at the ranch Moore outfitted me for a trip to New Mexico after ''Billy the Kid,'' and LX cattle which he and his gang had been stealing.

I finally started up the river with four large mules hitched to a heavy mess-wagon, with Francisco as driver and cook. My fighting crew consisted of five men: Big-foot Wallace, (Frank Clifford) Jim East, Cal Polk, Lon Chambers and Lee Hall.

In Tascosa we were joined by the Littlefield crew, in charge of Bob Roberson. He had a mess-wagon, a cook, and five riders.

We started out with only one horse apiece, with the exception of myself; I had two.

As corn was scarce it was thought best to buy more horses if we should need them.

On reaching San Lorenzo, New Mexico, I boarded a buck-board to Las Vegas, to buy a supply of corn, grub and ammunition, giving the outfit instructions to lay over in Anton Chico, on the Pecos river, until I got there.

I found Las Vegas to be a swift dance-hall town, and the first night of my arrival I went broke, playing monte—a Mexican game. I blowed in all my expense money, about $300, and about $100 which Bob Roberson had given me to buy ammunition and grub.

A big-hearted merchant by the name of Houton, or Van Houton, gave me the goods I needed, he taking orders on the LX company for pay.

On reaching Anton Chico with the wagon load of supplies, I learned that "Billy the Kid" and gang had slipped into town one night and stolen some fresh horses. They had come from the White Oaks country, to the south-westward.

We finally pulled out for White Oaks, and the next morning early, Pat Garrett, the sheriff of Lincoln County, New Mexico, rode into our camp. He said he was making up a crowd to go down the Pecos river in search of "Billy the Kid" and gang.

After consulting together, Bob Roberson and I decided to furnish Garrett part of our crew. Hence I turned over to him Lee Hall, Jim East, and Lon Chambers. Roberson loaned him Tom Emory and Louis Bozeman, Frank Stewart also joined Pat Garrett, he being his own boss and not subject to Roberson's orders.

In Anton Chico, Pat Garrett picked up a few of

his own men, his brother-in-law, Barney Mason being one of them. They then started down the Pecos river.

In the Mexican village of Puerto de Luna, Garrett proved his bravery. A drunken Mexican enemy fired a shot at him from the open door of a saloon, Garrett remarked that he didn't want to kill the fellow, so he would just break his right arm. This he did with a well aimed shot.

Roberson and I struck out for White Oaks in a raging snow storm.

When within a days ride of White Oaks we came to the still smoking ruins of the Jim Greathouse road-ranch, a saloon and store.

Here a posse from White Oaks, under the leadership of deputy-sheriff Jim Carlyle, fought a battle, a few days previous, with "Billy the Kid" and his gang.

While the posse had the gang surrounded in the Greathouse ranch, Jim Carlyle went in to have a talk with the "Kid."

For an hour or more the gang held Carlyle a prisoner, waiting for darkness to come so they could make their escape. They made him drink with them at the bar, every time they took a drink.

Finally Jim Carlyle jumped through a window to make his escape. As he sprang through the window the "Kid" shot him. He fell on the outside and began crawling away. Then the "Kid" killed him with another shot from his pistol.

In the darkest part of the night the gang made a break for liberty, and escaped.

The next day the posse set fire to the ranch, as it had become a rendezvous for outlaws.

In following the gang's trail through the snow they came to the Spence ranch, where the gang had eaten breakfast.

Now the posse burnt up Mr. Spence's buildings for feeding them.

By tramping all that day and part of the night the "Kid" gang reached Anton Chico, where they stole horses and saddles, while my outfit was there waiting for me to return from Las Vegas.

We arrived in the new mining camp of White Oaks in a severe snow storm.

For a week we camped out in the open with the snow nearly two feet deep, then we rented a building to live in.

Two of the leading merchants. Mr. Whiteman, and Mr. Sweet, gave us unlimited credit for grub and horse feed. We concluded to make this our headquarters until Pat Garrett and crowd were heard from. He had felt sure that he would find "Billy the Kid" and gang down on the Pecos river.

White Oaks was only a year old, but she contained over a thousand population, mostly venturesome men from all parts of the land, who flocked there after the first find of rich gold ore.

An outlaw by the name of Wilson had put

White Oaks on the map by stumbling onto a rich gold lead. He was making his get-away from Texas law officers, and cut across the county of Lincoln, New Mexico.

At White Oaks spring his pony played out, and seeing a smoke from a cabin three miles down the gulch he headed for it.

This cabin proved to be the home of two old California placer miners, Jack Winters, and John Wilson. They were washing gold out of the bed of Baxter Gulch, and hauling water on burros from White Oaks Spring.

The ground was rich in gold, and they generally took the gold dust to Lincoln, the county seat of Lincoln County, every Saturday, returning to Baxter Gulch on Mondays.

These two old prospectors gave outlaw Wilson permission to make himself at home in their cabin until his pony rested.

On the day after his arrival, after eating dinner, Wilson started out to walk to the top of Baxter Mountain, to view the surrounding country. He took a pick on his shoulder, telling the old prospectors that he might find a gold mine.

When half way up the high mountain, Wilson sat down on a boulder to rest. While resting he began to chip pieces off this quartz boulder.

When ready to proceed on his journey he picked up a large chip from this boulder, and seeing specks of yellow in it, he stuck it in his pocket.

It was almost dark when he got back to the cabin. Jack Winters was cooking flap-jacks for supper, on the sheet-iron stove. As a joke he asked Wilson if he had found a gold mine. He replied that he had found a rock with specks of yellow in it. He then handed Winters the chip from his pocket.

One glance at the rock sent Winters up in the air with a yell. This brought John Wilson out of his slumber, then he, too, became excited.

It required a lot of persuasion to get Wilson to go back up the mountain and show them the boulder from which this chip was broken. His argument being that he was worn out from his long tramp, and that the boulder would be there in the morning.

Finally the three started up the mountain side with lantern and location stakes, the flap-jacks being left on the stove to burn up.

On reaching the boulder, other similar quartz boulders were found further up the mountain, finally, by the light from the lantern, the quartz lead about three feet wide, was discovered. In picking into it wires of free gold were discovered.

Now the two old prospectors wrote out location notices on the stakes brought along. Wilson was asked his full name, so that he could be put in as a third owner. But he told them to locate it for themselves, as he had no use for a gold mine. Therefore two full claims, each 1500 feet in length and 600 feet in width, were located, running north and south, they being named the North Home-stake, and the South Homestake, Winters claimed the former and John Wilson the latter.

It was midnight when the three tired and hun-gry men returned to the cabin, and finished the flap-jack operation.

In a few days outlaw Wilson mounted his rested pony, and headed north-westward for the adobe village of Albuquerque, on the Rio Grande River, a distance of about 140 miles. He was pre-sented with an old pistol and 9 silver dollars, all the cash in camp, when he started.

Shortly after his departure officers from Texas arrived on Wilson's trail, but whether they ever over-took him is a question, as he had several days the start.

Shortly before our arrival in White Oaks, Jack Winters and John Wilson had sold the North and South Homestake to a St. Louis Company—each receiving $300,000 for their rich claims.

During one of his sober spells Jack Winters told me the story as outlined above.

This sudden fortune was too much for poor old Winters. Whiskey killed him within a year. In the last days of his life he gave a young lady—Miss B—$20,000 to care for him until he died.

Soon after the discovery of the Homestake mines two other rich leads were located at the foot of Baxter Mountain. One of them being the

Old Abe, and the other the Little Mack. The lat-
ter was secured in its infancy by Mr. Geo. W.
Prichard, now one of the leading lawyers of Santa
Fe, New Mexico, and the Old Abe by Mr. John Y.
Hewett, still a citizen of White Oaks.

Within a few years Mr. Hewett and his associates took out over $1,000,000 from the Old Abe
gold mine, the shaft now being down into the bow-
els of the earth over 1000 ft., and as dry as a bone,
no water having been struck, which is something
unusual.

Previous to our arrivel in White Oaks two
cowboys had a duel with pistols in the Bill Hudg-
ins Pioneer Saloon.

After the shooting was over Joe Fowler ran
into the saloon and asked the bar-keeper who fired
those shots. He pointed to the cowboy lying in
one corner of the saloon, badly wounded, as one
of the shooters. Then Joe Fowler pulled his pistol and shot the wounded cowboy dead. He then
made up a crowd and followed the other one to
White Oaks Springs, where they hung him to a
tree.

A few years later Joe Fowler was hanged by a
vigilance committee, in the town of Socorro, New
Mexico.

Fowler had just sold out his ranch and cattle in
Socorro County, for $50,000 and was in Socorro on
a spree. While on this spree he stabbed one of his
own cowboys to death. A short time previous he

had killed Jim Greathouse, (the man whose road house had been burnt by the White Oaks posse after the battle with "Billy the Kid") with a shot-gun, while he lay in bed.

This vigilante crowd allowed Fowler to have a fair jury trial. He had employed Tom Catron, and Thornton, of Santa Fe, to defend him.

When the jury brought in a verdict of guilty the vigilantes hung Fowler to a tree.

Before coming to New Mexico Joe Fowler own-ed a small cattle ranch in western Texas. He sold out to a friend of mine, now living in Alamogordo, New Mexico.

Soon after purchasing the ranch the new owner dug a ditch near the well, to put in a pipe line. In doing so the bodies of several men were dug up—victims, no doubt, of Fowlers murderous instinct.

At midnight our crowd ushered in the new year of 1881, in front of our picket shack. Each man emptied a Winchester rifle and a six-shooter in rapid succession. This being done to frighten the citizens of White Oaks, as we figured that they would think "Billy the Kid" had struck town. He had shot up the town a short time previous.

Our guess was correct for it caused a regular stampede out of the saloons and billiard-hall. The town marshal, "Pinto Tom," was playing bil-liards when the shooting began. He dropped his cue and broke for the back door, and took to the tall timber on the side of Carrizozo Mountain. It was noon next day when he returned. We had a man watching "Pinto Tom" to see what his actions would be.

Bob Roberson and I kept the neighbors around our shack supplied with fresh beef. A large steer would be dressed and hung up in a tree near by. The neighbors would help themselves to this stolen beef—so that we had to butcher a fresh one quite often. One of these beef eating neighbors, William C. McDonald, then a young surveyor, was the first governor of the state of New Mexico. He had become a wealthy cattle man, and was opposed to people eating stolen beef, but I reminded him of the time when he seemed to relish it. He made a splendid governor, and when he died, and was buried in White Oaks, a short time ago, I lost one of my dearest friends.

Roberson and I didn't consider that we were stealing, as in Texas it was the custom to kill anyone's animals for beef.

Most of the fat steers butchered by our crowd belonged to Tom Catron, later U. S. Senator, and his nephew, Mr. Waltz. They owned a cattle ranch at Carrizozo Springs—near where the prosperous little city of Carrizozo now stands.

The first word we had of "Billy the Kid" was when three of our boys, Lee Hall, Lon Chambers and Louis Boseman arrived from Ft. Sumner, with the news that "Billy the Kid" and gang had been captured, two of the gang being killed.

They explained the fight as follows:

On arriving in Ft. Sumner, Garrett learned that the "Kid" and his gang had been there and rode east for Portales Lake. Hence the sheriff surmised that they would soon return. Therefore camp was pitched in an old vacated adobe house, fronting the Ft. Sumner and Los Portales road.

In front of this house there was an adobe fence, behind which one man was put on guard every night to give the alarm if men were seen coming toward Ft. Sumner.

Several nights later while Lon Chambers was on duty, behind the adobe fence, a crowd of men was seen by the moonlight coming down the road.

Chambers at once gave the alarm to Garrett and the boys who were playing poker. Then all lined themselves along the adobe fence.

When the man in the lead was opposite, Garrett stood up and called to him to throw up his hands. Instead he drew his pistol, and received several bullets through the body. These shots scattered the gang like a flock of quail. Many shots were fired at them as they took the back-track, from whence they had come.

The dead man proved to be Tom O'Phalliard. He breathed a few times after being carried into the house.

Now Garrett and posse took up the trail in the deep snow, after daylight.

Twelve miles out they came to a dead horse, which had been wounded in the stomach the night previous.

From now on two of the gang were mounted on one pony, which made their progress slow.

Towards midnight that night a one-room rock house loomed up ahead, and the trail in the snow ended there, showing that the gang were inside the cabin.

Now the posse rode behind a high hill and built a fire.

Just before daylight Pat Garrett and Lee Hall walked to the cabin afoot. They lay down along the west wall, near the corner, from whence the door could be covered with their rifles. Outside of this door stood four shivering ponies, the ropes around their necks being on the inside.

At the first peep of day one man walked out of the cabin, and the sheriff commanded him to throw up his hands. He jumped back towards the door, and received two bullets through the body. Then with his hands up he walked to Garrett and Hall saying: "I wish, I wish!" and fell over dead. This man proved to be Charlie Bowdre.

Now the gang inside began pulling one of the ponies inside through the door-way. When half way in Garrett sent a bullet through the pony's heart. This blocked up the entrance.

"Billy the Kid" already had his little race mare inside, and it was their intention to pull the balance of the ponies inside, and then make a dash out of the door-way for liberty.

Now the sheriff and the "Kid" opened up a conversation, they passed jokes back and forth.

There were no windows in the cabin, and the gang tried to pick portholes through the thick stone walls, with their guns and knives, but this proved a failure.

All that day and the following night the gang held out without food, water or fire.

The next day they decided to surrender. "Billy the Kid" was the last to come out with hands up. There were only four of them left: Billy Wilson, Tom Picket, Rudabaugh, and the "Kid."

On arrival in Ft. Sumner the sheriff sent part of our boys to White Oaks, while he took Jim East, Tom Emory, and Frank Stewart with him to the railroad, at Las Vegas. There they boarded a train for Santa Fe, where the prisoners were put in the penitentiary for safe-keeping.

In Las Vegas a mob was formed to hang "Billy the Kid," but they were stood off until the train could pull out.

After the return of Tom Emory and Jim East, Bob Roberson decided, as the "Kid" was behind prison walls, to return home. I had concluded to stay until Spring, and gather up any LX cattle that might be in the country.

As Jim East wished to return to Tascosa, and run for sheriff of Oldham County, Texas, I allowed him to go back with the Roberson crowd. I also let Lee Hall and Cal Polk go. As Tom Emory wished to stay with me Roberson gave his consent.

At that time none of us knew that Tom Emory was an escaped convict from the penitentiary in Huntsville, Texas, under an assumed name.

About thirty years later Emory's wealthy brother in Texas made a deal with the Governor to grant him a pardon. It was necessary that Tom **go** back to prison, in order to be pardoned. He spent one night in the penitentiary and then went to live with his brother. He afterwards died.

I finally received several hundred dollars of expense money from Mr. Moore, with orders to stay in the country as long as I wished.

We continued to feed our neighbors stolen beef —not exactly stolen, but butchered according to the Texas custom.

Well do I remember of "Shanghai" Pierce once riding into our camp, when one of his animals was being butchered; he said: "Boys, the day is coming when every man will have to eat his own beef." That day came before we old-time cowboys had time to realize it.

About the first of February I took Tom Emory with me and rode to Ft. Stanton to examine the hides in Pat Cohglin's slaughter house there, he

having the contract to furnish the soldiers with
beef.

Emory was mounted on his grey horse, while
I rode one of the work mules, a dandy saddle animal.

We first went to the town of Lincoln and secured the services of Johnny Hurley—afterwards
killed by outlaws—as a witness in case we found
any LX hides at Ft. Stanton.

In searching the Cohglin slaughter house, in
charge of "Old Papen" we found many LX hides
—some freshly butchered. These were taken and
stored.

Now I decided to see the "King of Tularosa,"
as Pat Cohglin was called, and warn him not to
kill any more LX cattle.

From Ft. Stanton we rode over the White
Mountains to the Mescalero Apache Agency, then
in charge of Major Wm. H. H. Llewellin, now a
prominent lawyer of Las Cruces, New Mexico.

Here Major Llewellin told of John S——passing through the agency a short time previous,
with a herd of Texas cattle, bound for the west.
The fact of the herd being driven in a hurry, and
through deep snow, made it look as though they
might be stolen cattle. Hence I concluded to follow their trail.

On arriving in Tularosa one night I attended a
Mexican fandango, (dance) and found a Mexican
who had piloted the John S— —herd across the

"White Sands." I had him mark out some of the brands on paper. Among them he drew the LX brand, which made me more determined to stay on the trail.

At the Cohglin store in Tularosa I learned that Pat Cohglin had gone west on trail of 300 of his cattle, stolen by Tom Cooper, one of "Billy the Kid's" gang.

Here I sent Tom Emory back to White Oaks to tell the boys to lay there until my return. Then a young Texan, by the name of Sam Coleman, and I started across the "White Sands" desert, for Las Cruces, on the Rio Grande. I had met Coleman in Texas. He was now going to Arizona to grow up with the country, which he did.

Arriving in Las Cruces I found the "King of Tularosa," returning from his unsuccessful chase after Tom Cooper. He was a large, fine looking old Irishman, with the "ould sod" love for red "licker."

On telling him of finding the LX hides in his slaughter house, and of my intentions to search his range for LX cattle on my return, he promised not to butcher any more, If I would wait until April the first before rounding up his cattle, as he didn't want them disturbed until grass became green in the spring. I promised, not realizing he was playing a "dirty Irish trick" on me.

Now I spent a few days in Las Cruces, under an assumed name, working in with the notorious

"Hurricane Bill," and his tough gang, to find out more about the John S—— herd of cattle. I had learned that "Hurricane Bill" had just arrived from Tombstone, Arizona. On making his acquaintance he told me of this John S—— herd having arrived in Tombstone before his departure from there.

"Hurricane Bill" and his chum, "Baldy" Johnson, wanted me to join their gang. They said they were making big money stealing cattle, and selling them to Johnny Kinney who ran a slaughter house in Rincon, forty miles above Las Cruces, then the terminus of the Atchison, Topeka and Santa Fe railroad, building south into El Paso.

Later I met this Johnny Kinney and he invited me to accompany him to a swell Mexican wedding in La Mesilla, three miles from Las Cruces. This Mexican wedding gave me my first champagne headache.

Now I wrote to Mr. Moore about the John S—— herd, and advised him to send a good man to Tombstone, Arizona, by rail and stage, to investigate the matter. He sent John W. Poe, a deputy U. S. Marshall from Ft. Elliot, Texas. But when he arrived in Tombstone the John S—— herd had been sold and scattered to the four winds of Heaven—hence Mr. Poe had his trip for nothing.

I started back to White Oaks. One night was spent in Tularosa. The next morning I started for

the Pat Cohglin cattle ranch on Three Rivers—
now the property of U. S. Senator A. B. Fall—a
distance of twenty miles.

On the way there I met a lone horse-man. He
introduced himself to me as Johnny Reily. Thirty
five years later I was reading a magazine, on the
front porch of the De Vargas Hotel, in Santa Fe,
when an old gentleman passed me on his way into
the hotel. I looked up, and our eyes met. He
said: "Say, didn't I meet you in 1881 on the road
between Tularosa and Three Rivers?"

I mention this to show the fine memory of some
human beings.

Now Johnny Reily, the wealthy cattle man re-
siding in the El Paso Club at Colorado Springs,
Colorado, sat down beside me to "hark back" to
the bloody Lincoln County war, in which he took
a prominent part.

He told of one incident to show the cheap re-
gard for human life in that noted war. He said
he and Jimmie Dolan owned a store near Ft. Stanton, and had been at war with "Billy the Kid" and
his crowd. One night the "Kid" and some of his
warriors pitched camp in the hills near their
store.

Early the next morning the "Kid" sent one of
his men to the store with a peace treaty to be
signed by Reily and Dolan.

After the paper was signed they all went across
the road to a saloon, to take a drink. A drummer

from the east, who had just sold them a bill of goods, accompanied them to the saloon.

While filling the glasses to take a drink the traveling man criticised "Billy the Kid" and his lawless bunch. Here "Billy the Kid's" man told him to keep quiet, as he was not in the civilized east. He replied that as an American citizen he had a right to criticise lawlessness.

He hadn't more than finished the sentence when the "Kid" man shot him dead, Reily said he and Dolan started to run to the door, but the fellow leveled his pistol at them saying: "Finish your drink, boys, don't let a little thing like this excite you". They finished the drink, and were glad to get back to the store alive.

At the Pat Cohglin ranch I put up for the night, and was royally treated by Mr. and Mrs. George Nesbeth, the couple who looked after the cooking and ranch work. A Mexican was in charge of the live-stock.

During the evening Mr. and Mrs. Nesbeth told me of how they were present when Pat Cohglin made a deal with "Billy the Kid" to buy all the Panhandle, Texas, cattle that he could steal and deliver to him at Three Rivers.

The next morning when ready to start for White Oaks, by way of the wagon road, around the mountains, the Mexican foreman told me that I could save ten miles by taking a trail over the high mountain range. He agreed to send one of his Mexican cowboys to put me on the right trail.

Accepting his kind offer we started.

When about five miles up the mountain side a plain trail was struck, and the pilot returned towards home.

About an hour later the trail made a bend to the left, and to save time I cut across to strike it further up the mountain. This move, no doubt, saved my life, as assassins were laying for me a short distance ahead on the trail.

Finally three shots were fired in quick succession, and my mule lunged forward, slipping on the ice covered ground. She fell on her side throwing me over an eight foot cliff. My pistol was hanging to the saddle-horn, but it was grabbed and pulled out of the scabbard as I went off the saddle.

With the pistol ready for action I lay quiet for a few moments, thinking the would-be assassins might show up. I then crawled up the cliff just in time to see two men running over a ridge, a few hundred yards distant. They were afoot, and only in sight a minute. No doubt they thought I was killed, and were running back to where their mounts had been left.

The mule was found a couple of hundred yards up the mountain with her front leg fast in the bridle-rein. The ground was covered with blood, which had flown from the wound in her breast.

On investigation I found that one bullet had

ploughed a furrow through the hind tree of my saddle, and another went through a blanket tied behind the saddle.

The mule was not badly wounded, hence I reached White Oaks about dark, after an absence of about two weeks.

Over thirty years later my cowboy friend, John P. Meadows, of Tularosa, new Mexico, told me the secret of this attempted assassination. He had learned the facts in the case from Mexicans living at Three Rivers. Pat Cohglin had paid them to kill me, to prevent prosecution for the LX hides found in his slaughter house.

At this writing John P. Meadows is the owner of the Cohglin block in Tularosa, he having acquired it after Cohglins death, a few years ago.

For the next month we took life easy in the lively town of White Oaks, and continued to eat fresh beef. The only brand we looked for, in selecting an animal for slaughter, was fat.

The town supported a weekly newspaper, The Golden Era, hence we kept posted on local affairs. One of the boys then on the Golden Era force, Emerson Hough, has attained a world-wide reputation as a writer.

Soon after my return to camp "Big-foot Wallace" (Frank Clifford) and I rode out in the hills to get a steer for slaughter. He was butchered in the edge of town, and the cook, Francisco, hauled the meat to our quarters in the mess-wagon.

On entering our picket shack, one of the boys told "Big-foot Wallace" that the town school master, Sheldon, was hunting him with a gun, to settle a difficulty they had got into that morning.

".Big foot" had just sat down to eat his supper. Jumping up he remarked: "Well I will go and hunt him!" So saying he pulled his Colts pistol out of the scabbard, lying on the floor, and stuck it in his right boot. Then he started down town. I tried to persuade him to wait until after supper, when I would go with him, but he was too angry to wait.

Soon we heard six shots fired in quick succession, and a moment later, two louder shots.

Jumping on my pony bare-back I ran down town. Finding "Bog-foot" surrounded by a big crowd of men, I advised him to jump on, behind me, on the pony's back and return to camp, which he did.

He explained matters by saying that he met Sheldon and another man walking up the street towards him. On meeting, he asked Sheldon if he was hunting for him.

Now Sheldon drew a pocket pistol and opened fire. "Big-foot" reached down to his boot-top to get his gun, but found that the leg of his pants had slipped down over the gun.

By the time he got the pants leg up, and the pistol out, Sheldon had emptied his pistol and was running down the street. Just as he turned a corner "Big-foot" fired two shots at him, one of them knocking a button off his coat, and putting a hole in it.

None of Sheldon's bullets had hit the target.

The next morning "Big-foot" received a summons from Justice of the Peace Frank Lea, to appear in his Court, on the charge of attempted murder, at 10 a. m.

We all mounted and rode down town. I employed lawyer John Y. Hewett—still a resident of White Oaks—to defend "Big-foot."

There were five of us in the crowd, and we wore our six-shooters and bowie-knives into the court room.

"Pinto Tom," the town marshall, demanded that we take off our fire-arms while court was in session. This request was refused, then he called on Judge Lea to make us put up the guns.

Now I called "Pinto Tom" to step outside with me, which he did. There I told him that he was committing suicide, as the boys were ready to fill him full of holes if he persisted any further. This settled the matter, and the case proceeded. "Big-foot" was cleared of the charge.

Sheldon was never arrested for his part in the shooting scrape—possibly because he did such poor shooting, which convinced Judge Lea that he was harmless.

Two years later poor Sheldon was hung by a

mob in Socorro, on the Rio Grande river. He had been thrown into jail to sober up, that night.

The only other occupants of the jail were young Ethan Allen, of White Oaks, and a negro. Towards morning a mob of Mexicans broke into the jail and liberated the negro, hanging young Allen and the White Oaks school-master to a near by tree. This was done to spite the "Gringoes" (Americans) for hanging the Baca brothers a short time previous.

On the night before the hanging of Sheldon, "Big-foot" Wallace and Ethan Allen had held up and robbed a big store in Los Lunas, near Socorro. "Big-foot made his escape by swimming the raging Rio Grande river, amidst a shower of bullets from the law-officers. Ethan Allen being captured, and thrown in jail with Sheldon and the negro.

"Big-foot" reached Old Mexico, and made his home there until a few years ago when he was shot and killed, according to the reports received by me.

On reaching Old Mexico "Big-foot" wrote me a letter, enclosing his photograph, which is retained as a relic of the wild and wooly cattle days.

Finally I received a confidential letter from Mr. George Nesbeth, on the Pat Cohglin ranch, stating that Mr. Cohglin was not keeping the promise made to me, not to butcher any more LX cattle. The letter went on to state that he was trying to get them all butchered before the first of April.

Now I got busy and sent Emory and Chambers
to three Rivers with the mess-wagon, while ''Big-
foot'' and I rode to Ft. Stanton to search the Cohglin slaughter house. We found five freshly butchered LX hides—the ones previously butchered
having evidently been hauled off and hidden.

From Ft. Stanton we made a hard ride over the
White Mountains for the Cohglin ranch, arriving
there in the night.

Mr. and Mrs. Nesbeth got up out of bed and
cooked us a warm meal.

Early next morning the balance of my outfit arrived, then we cut out five large LX steers from
Bill Gentry's herd. Gentry, the foreman, refused
to give them up without orders from Pat Cohglin.
But we told him that if he wanted war we were
ready. He had seven Mexican cowboys with him.

Now we spent three days rounding up the Cohglin range, only finding three more LX steers.
Then we returned to White Oaks, taking with us
one of Cohglin's fattest steers, which was butchered in White Oaks for the benefit of our meat-
loving friends there.

Now we started towards home, rounding up
cattle on small ranches through the Patos Mountains, then the Van Sickle range, now the large
Block ranch, on the north side of Capitan Mountains.

From here we went to Los Palos Springs, where

the tough little town of Arabella now stands. Thence to Roswell, on the Pecos River.

Roswell was a town with two stores, one owned by that whole-souled Missourian, Capt. J. C. Lea, a bother of Judge Frank Lea of White Oaks, and the other by a Mr. Cosgrove.

Here we laid over a week to wait until John Chisum started the spring round-up on his "Jingle-bob" range, containing about 60,000 cattle.

During this time we attended dances on Pumpkin Row, where a bunch of Texans had settled a few miles south of Roswell.

At his home ranch, on south Spring River, John Chisum had built a new frame dwelling, under which flowed a sparkling irrigation stream to water the young orchard just planted.

On the front porch if this new house I used to sit for hours talking to Cattle King John Chisum. His whole heart seemed wrapped up in this large young orchard. It is now the home of Ex-Governor Herbert J. Hagerman—hence Mr. Chisum planted the orchard for others to enjoy, as he died a few years later.

When the Chisum round-up started south to the Texas line, a distance of nearly 200 miles, to begin rounding up to brand calves, we followed.

I left Tom Emory in Roswell to guard our small bunch of steers. He made his home with Capt. J. C. Lea, and during the daytime grazed

the steers on the grassy flat in front of the Lea
Store. Now that grassy flat is covered with large
business blocks, with paved streets, as Roswell
has grown to be an up-to-date little city, with
about 7,000 population.

On our way down the Pecos River we camped
for dinner one day, on the west bank of the stream
—near where the little city of Carlsbad is now located.

The river was bank-full from melted snow at its
head. We were sitting on the ground near the
water's edge, with plates on our laps, eating dinner, when a man rode up on a black horse, he
said: "Say, boys, did you hear the news?"

When I replied "No." he continued:

"Billy the Kid" has killed his two guards in
Lincoln and escaped."

At that moment "Big-foot Wallace" gave a
Comanche Indian yell, saying: "Hurrah for
"Billy the Kid " Then he dived headlong into
the muddy water of the Pecos. He had on his
boots, spurs, leather leggins and six-shooter, with
a belt of cartridges. When he came to the surface
he yelled again: "hurrah for the Kid." Then he
swam ashore and wrung the water from his
clothes.

This stranger didn't know the full particulars
of the "Kid's" escape, but on our return to Roswell, two weeks later, we found out all about it.

We finally started up the river with our ten LX

steers, having found two near the Chisum home ranch.

Six miles above the abandoned Post of Ft. Sumner, at Sunnyside, I went ahead with the mess-wagon to buy horse-feed and grub.

On riding up to the platform, in front of the store, I dismounted, and pulling my Winchester rifle out of the saddle scabbard I walked into the open door. I had lost a screw out of the rifle, and wanted to buy another that would fit.

As I entered the door several men went running out of the rear entrance. There was no one left in the store but the proprietor, who seemed greatly excited. He said: "Well, I'll be d——d! we thought you was "Billy the Kid." You look just like him. "Then the store man went to the rear entrance and called out: "Come back boys, its a false alarm."

Others had previously told me that I looked like "Billy the Kid." Now I felt convinced that it must be true.

These men had heard of "Billy the Kid's escape, after killing his two guards.

I then returned to Ft. Sumner and laid over to attend a Mexican dance that night.

Mrs. Charlie Bowdre—whose husband was killed by Pat Garrett and Lee Hall—attended this dance. She being a good-looking young Mexican woman, I danced with her often.

When the dance broke up before daylight I

accompanied Mrs. Bowdre to her two-room adobe
house. I tried to persuade her to allow me to go
inside and talk awhile. Then I bade her goodnight.

On meeting her the coming fall she told me the
reason for her not letting me enter the house. That
"Billy the Kid" was in hiding there, at the time.
Now we struck out east for Portales Lake, on
the west edge of the Staked Plains.

We camped one night at Stinking Springs, and
slept in the rock house where "Billy the Kid" and
his gang held out for about two days and nights,
without fire, food or water.

Lon Chambers and Tom Emory pointed out to
"Big-foot" and me the spot where Charlie Bow-
dre fell, when hit by bullets from Garrett's and
Hall's rifles.

The stone walls inside showed the marks of
where the gang tried to pick port-holes.

Arriving at Los Portales Lake—near where the
thriving county-seat town of Portales, New
Mexico, is now located—we pitched camp at "Billy
the Kid's cave." It was here at a large fresh water spring—the lake being salty—that the "Kid"
and gang made their headquarters, while stealing
LX steers for Pat Cohglin.

This "cave" was not a cave—just an overhanging rock cliff, with a stone corral around it, on
three sides.

A few years later this "cave" and fresh water
spring were taken up, as a small cattle ranch, by

a cowboy friend of mine, Doak Good. He afterwards killed a man, which broke him up in business, as it took his small bunch of cattle to pay lawyers fees, and other costs in the case.

From now on our misery began, gathering Canadian River cattle, which in past winters had strayed away, drifting south with the buffalo. They had become as wild as deer.

Being short of horses we had to press the four work mules into service, to stand night-watch over the cattle.

Further east there was a chain of fresh water lakes, on the head draws of the Yellow-house canyon, a tributary of the Brazos River, and around them we found many cattle.

After leaving these lakes we were two days and nights without water.

The first habitation we struck, since leaving Ft. Sumner, was Walter Dyer's log house on the head of Paladuro Canyon, a distance of about 200 miles.

Now over that same stretch of country dwell thousands of prosperous "fool-hoe-men," and their happy families.

The chances are some of these settlers, east of Los Portales Lake, found the remains of a twelve year old boy, and counted it as another unsolved mystery of the Llano Estacado.

In the fall of 1887 Bill McCoy, a Panhandle

cowboy, whom I knew as Bill Gatlin, shot and killed deputy sheriff Gunn, of Lusk, Wyoming. He
was tried and sentenced to hang for the crime.
Just before he was to be hanged, Tom Nichols,
alias Tom Hall, foreman of the Keeline cattle
ranch on the Larmie river, in Wyoming, paid a
tough eastern safe-blower $500.00 to liberate Mc-
Coy. He committed a petty crime in Cheyenne and
was thrown in jail. Then his time was spent with
steel saws, concealed in the soles of his shoes, to
liberate the prisoners.

On the night of the liberation Tom Hall was at
a designated place, with an extra horse and saddle
to take McCoy to the Keeline ranch, where he was
kept hidden out for a while.

Finally McCoy pulled out with two good horses, going through the state of Utah into New
Mexico.

In Utah he picked up a twelve year old boy who
wanted to be a cowboy outlaw. He was allowed to
ride the extra horse.

On arriving in Santa Fe their mounts were
played out. Gatlin then hired a buggy and team to
drive out in the country. When a few miles out
of the city the saddles were put onto the buggy
horses, and a hard ride made to the Los Portales
Lake, where then lived Len Woodruff, a former
LX cowboy.

Gatlin and Woodruff were warm friends, as
more than once they "shot up" the town of Tas-

cosa together. In one of these shootings Len Woodruff was shot all to pieces—being made a cripple for life.

Bill Gatlin told Woodruff that he had foolishly confessed to this boy, that he was under sentence of death, and for that reason he wanted to "shake" him.

They had tried to persuade the boy to quit Gatlin, as he didn't want him with him, but he wouldn't listen to the advice. He said Gatlin had promised to take him to South America and that he had to keep his promise.

Woodruff kept the boy in the tent until Gatlin had been gone about half an hour. Then he was turned loose, as he had promised to make his home with Len Woodruff.

Now Woodruff went to work about his chores. Soon he looked to the south-westward and saw the boy on his horse running on Gatlin's trail.

Two days later, while out hunting lost horses, Woodruff found this boy's horse and saddle. The saddle was covered with blood.

When telling me this story Woodruff said he felt sure Gatlin had shot the boy from his horse, after he had overtaken him, (Gatlin).

I was already familiar with this Bill McCoy murder case, as the district attorney, Walter Stoll, of Cheyenne, Wyoming, had employed me as a detective to investigate the matter.

As a supposed Texas outlaw I spent a couple of months on the Keeline ranch.

I traced Bill McCoy to New Orleans where he shipped on a sailing vessel for Buenos Ayres, South America—thence 1200 miles onto the Pampas, where he joined a gang of Texas outlaws, some of them being chums of Tom Hall.

In a few years Gatlin became tired of South America and returned to the United States. He finally settled down and married in south-western New Mexico, where he raised a family, and became a well-to-do cattle man.

The chances are Bill Gatlin, alias Bill McCoy, would sweat blood did he know that I knew his present name and address, for the hangman's noose would stare him in the face.

If he really did kill that boy he should be hanged more than once.

We arrived at the LX ranch on the 22nd day of June, with 2500 head of cattle, after an absence of seven months.

CHAPTER VIII.

A 3000 MILE HORSE-BACK RIDE.
A TRUE ACCOUNT OF "BILLY THE KID'S" ESCAPE, AND DEATH.

On returning to the ranch I found that we had no boss, as Mr. Moore had quit to look after his own cattle.

Mr. David T. Beals, who was at the Ranch, complimented me on my seven months work. He said, on the strtngth of my letters, they had sent John W. Poe to Lincoln County, New Mexico, to prosecute Pat Cohglin.

Mr. Beals presented me with a fine-blooded colt, which I afterwards sold for $200 to the Reverend Carhart, of Clarendon. He also promised me that when his company met, to select a new manager for the LX ranch, he would present my name, and recommend me for the position.

John Hollicott, a slow, easy-going Scotch cowboy was selected as general manager of the ranch, to take Moore's place, a few months later.

Mr. Beals told me that other members of his company objected to me, as being too wild and reckless for such a responsible position.

As the "fool hoe-men" were settling the country around Mobeta, Mr. Beals began buying up all land on the LX range, which bordered on streams, or took in watering places, such as lakes and springs. But he was only allowed to purchase every two sections of land out of three. Every third section being State School Land, which could only be taken up by actual settlers. The State lands, and the Gunter & Munson sections, were for sale, and these constituted his purchases.

In the early 70s the State of Texas had made a deal with Gunter and Munson, of Sherman, Texas, to survey most of the Texas Panhandle. Their pay being a deed to every third section (640 acres) of land.

There being about twenty-five counties in the Panhandle, you can imagine the number of sections these two Sherman lawyers owned, after the survey was finished.

In the early '80's the state deeded 3,000,000 acres of land, adjoining New Mexico, to the "Merchant Prince," J. V. Farwell, and his Chicago associates, as pay for the erection of a new capitol building in Austin.

On this large tract of land the Capitol Syndicate established the XIT cattle ranch, which became one of the largest in the Panhandle.

When the "fool hoe-men" began to flock into the Panhandle, and land could be sold for $20 and more per acre, the Capitol Syndicate cut up their large holdings into small farms, cutting down the number of cattle accordingly.

I spent the balance of the summer in charge of a branding crew.

During the middle part of October a letter was received from John W. Poe, for Lon Chambers and me to be in Lincoln, New Mexico, to appear as witnesses against Pat Cohglin, on the 7th of November. Hence we had to hurry, as it meant a horse-back ride of about 600 miles.

I was instructed by Mr. Erskine Clement, who was in charge of outside matters, to put in the coming winter scouting along the Texas and Pacific railroad, at the foot of the South Staked Plains, in search of strayed LX cattle.

After a hard ride across country, part of the time without water, we reached Lincoln in the night, as per Mr. Poe's instructions, so that Pat Cohglin wouldn't know we were to appear as witnesses against him.

Mr. Poe had arranged for us to board with a Mr. Cline, twelve miles down the Hondo river, and keep in hiding until we were called as witnesses.

On arriving at the Cline ranch, about daylight, we received a hearty welcome from Mr. Cline and his Mexican family.

After being in hiding twelve days Mr. Poe rode down to tell us that Pat Cohglin had been granted a change of venue to Dona Ana County. He instructed me to be in La Mesilla, on the Rio Grande, the first Monday in April, 1882, to attend court. He told Lon Chambers that he could return home, as he would not be needed, which he did.

Now, mounted on "Croppy"—a milk-white horse with both ears frozen off close to his head —with "Buckshot" for a pack animal, I started for Roswell.

On arriving in Roswell I rode out a short distance to sheriff Pat Garrett's ranch, but found out that Mr. Garrett had gone to Dallas. Old man Ash Upson, who was living with the sheriff and his Mexican family, informed me that he had just re-

ceived a letter from Pat Garrett, with instructions to meet him at Pecos Station, on the T. P.
Ry. with the covered hack on a certain day.

Mr. Upson and I decided to make this nearly
two hundred miles trip together. He drove ahead
with his covered rig and I followed with my pack
outfit. But we pitched camp together at night.

In riding along one day I passed a covered
hack by the side of the road, and heard my name
called. Then I rode over to the camp, a few rods
distant, and found my friend, Clay Allison, the
man-killer. He introduced me to his new wife, a
young corn-fed Missouri girl.

Of course I had to lay over for the noon-day
lunch, so as to sample this Missouri Girl's cooking.

Mr. Allison was in search of a new location to
settle down. He selected a ranch near Seven Rivers, and started a small cattle ranch.

Several years later, while intoxicated, he fell off
a wagon and broke his neck. Thus did the killer of
eighteen men die with his boots on.

On Christmas Eve, Ash and I put up for the
night at the Jones ranch on Seven Rivers. Mr.
and Mrs. Jones were warm friends of Mr. Upson's
—hence they invited us to lay over Christmas and
eat turkey dinner with them, which we did. We
"shore" enjoyed the turkey, sweet-potatoes,
pumpkin pie and egg-nog.

On this trip Ash Upson told me the history of

"Billy the Kid"—whom he had known from childhood. His true name was Billy Bonney; he was born on the 23rd of November 1859, in New York City.

After his father's death, his mother married a Mr. Antrim, who soon after moved to Santa Fe, New Mexico, where Ash Upson was in the newspaper business.

In Santa Fe Mr. and Mrs. Antrim opened a restaurant, and had Mr. Upson as a boarder. The "Kid" then being only ten years old.

A few years later Ash Upson and Mr. Antrim moved to Silver City.

Soon after "Billy the Kid" went on a trip to Ft. Union, and killed his first man, a negro soldier.

On the LX ranch, in the fall of '78 the "Kid" told me that his first killing was a negro soldier in Ft. Union.

On returning to Silver City he killed a blacksmith in a personal encounter. Now he skipped out for Old Mexico to avoid arrest.

In the city of Chihuahua, Mexico, he killed and robbed a Mexican monte dealer.

He then "hit the high places" for Texas, finally arriving in Lincoln County, New Mexico, where he went to work for an Englishman by the name of Tunstall.

In the spring of 1878 a mob, headed by Morton, from the Rio Pecos, shot and killed Tunstall.

Now "Billy the Kid" swore that he would kill every man who had a hand in the murder of his friend, Tunstall. He made up a crowd of warriors consisting of Tom O'Phalliard, Henry Brown, Fred Wyatt, Sam Smith, Jim French, John Middleton, R. M. Bruer, J. G. Skurlock, Charlie Bowdre, Frank McNab and a fellow named McClosky, and started out to kill the murderers of Tunstall.

This was the starting of the bloody Lincoln County war. Before the war ended Morton and his crowd were killed.

Sheriff Brady undertook the job of breaking up the "Kid's" gang, and was killed by "Billy the Kid," He had shot him from behind an adobe wall, as he rode down the main street of Lincoln. As the sheriff lay in the road badly wounded "Billy the Kid" ran out from behind the adobe wall and shot him through the head.

Now the whole county became a battle-ground, many good Citizens joining the "Kid's" gang.

During this war "Billy the Kid" and a dozen of his men took refuge in lawyer McSween's residence in Lincoln. In the night they were surrounded by thirty-five "Seven River Warriors," and two companies of United States Soldiers, under command of Col. Dudley of the ninth cavalry.

The McSween residence was set afire. When the fire became too hot the "Kid" and his party dashed out of the kitchen door, shooting as they ran. "Billy the Kid" and Tom O'Phalliard were the only ones who escaped without a scratch. Lawyer McSween lay dead with nine bullets in his body.

Ash Upson had previously moved from Silver City to Lincoln County, hence he knew all about this local war.

Ash and I arrived   at Pecos station at three o'clock on New Years Eve. We had been traveling slowly, as Pat Garrett was not due to arrive at Pecos until after New Years.

There being no accomodations at Pecos station Ash and I concluded to board the evening westbound train for Toyah, twenty miles distant. Our horses being left in charge of a wolf-hunter.

In Toyah we put up at the Alvarado Hotel, owned by a Mr. Newell.

After supper Ash took in the town, while I remained at the hotel to enjoy the company of Mr. Newell's fifteen year old daughter, Miss Beulah.

About midnight Ash returned to the hotel loaded to his full capacity with fire-water, though he swore that he hadn't drunk anything but "Tom and Jerry."

On New Years morning a big shooting match for turkeys was to take place in the edge of town, Miss Beulah expressed a wish that someone bring her a fat bird. Of course that meant me, so I promised that she should have a few turkeys.

The Justice of the Peace, Mr. Miller, had sent

to Dallas for the turkeys, which had cost him $3 each.

When the shooting match started, a fat gobbler was put in an iron box, with only his head visible. The shooting to be done with pistols, off-hand, at a distance of thirty-five yards. Each shooter to pay twenty-five cents a shot, with a free shot to follow if he killed the turkey.

I paid my twenty-five cents and was put down as number eleven.

Ten men fired but the gobbler was still alive. Now my Colts 45 pistol was raised and off went the bird's head. Then another was put in the iron box, and his head went off, or at least fell over on the box.

Here Judge Miller said he would have to bar me out from shooting any more. He explained that he had a large family to support, and that he ought, at least, to get his money back for his flock of turkeys.

With the two gobblers on my shoulder I returned to the hotel and laid them at Miss Beulah's feet. Of course she thanked me.

From now on I was known as the "turkey shooter." Many times in riding along the railroad I was recognized by men on passing trains and hailed as the "turkey shooter." They knew my crop-eared horse.

That night we had a big turkey supper at the Alvarado Hotel, and a dance afterwards.

There were only two young ladies at the dance, Miss Beulah, and a Miss Lee. The balance being married ladies.

During the whole night shots could be heard down town, fired by hilarious cowboys and rail-roaders. Much of this shooting being over the heads of frightened Chinamen, there being about a dozen in town. They left for El Paso on the first train, and it was said that Pig-tails steered clear of Toyah ever afterwards.

A few days after New Years a telegram came to Ash from Pat Garrett, at Pecos Station, tell-ing him to come on the first train, as he was in a hurry to get home.

Ash being in bed drunk, he got me to answer the message, which read: "Can't leave here; owe every man in town."

Soon another message came; it stated: "If you don't come on the first train I will strike out and leave you."

This angered Mr. Upson, and he told me to write a reply just as dictated. With pencil in hand I wrote down the words, which were: "Go to, hic, h—l, d—m you."

On receiving this message the sheriff came up on the first train and paid Upson's debts, then took the old man back with him. I never saw poor Ash Upson afterwards, as he died a few years la-ter.

From Toyah I drifted east along the T. P. Ry.

onto the southern edge of the Staked Plains, leaving the rail-road at Sand Hill Station, and circling around to the north-eastward, to buffalo-hunters camps. It had been reported that as buffalo were getting scarce, stray cattle were being killed for their hides. But I satisfied myself that these reports were false.

At Cedar Lake I made the acquaintance of two noted buffalo hunters, the Whaley brothers. I afterwards met them in Big Springs, where they were waiting for the money from a shipment of buffalo hides.

When this money, $600, reached them they began drinking and gambling in Big Springs.

One night they were "bucking" monte—a Mexican game. The small red complected brother was sitting in a chair at the end of the table, while the other, a fine looking large man was up on the table, on his knees.

An argument arose about a twenty-five cent bet, which had won. The small man picked up the money, claiming it was his. Then the other brother pulled his pistol and shot him through the heart. As he was falling he jerked out his pistol and shot the other man through the body. He ran out on the street and fell over dead. Thus ended the career of two of the best known buffalo hunters on the Llano Estacado.

I finally landed in Colorado City, at the head of the Colorado River, flat broke.

Walking into the largest store in town I introduced myself to the proprietor, Mr. "Pete" Snyder, for whom the now prosperous town of Snyder, Texas, was named. I asked for the loan of
$50, until money from the LX ranch could reach
me. Without any 'hums or haws' he pulled out the
,amount and handed it to me. This shows the broad-
gauge spirit of these old-time westerners. When
my $200, post-office money-order, from Erskine
Clement, arrived I repaid Mr. Snyder.

I spent a couple of weeks riding over the large
range owned by Lum Slaughter of Dallas, Texas.

Now my face was turned westward for a 500
mile ride to La Mesilla, New Mexico, to attend
court.

In Big Springs I lay two days with a burning
fever. Realizing the importance of my presence
in court, I got up out of a sick bed and continued
my journey.

After dark, just as a cold norther and sleet
storm had sprung up, I rode up to a section house,
and called, "hello!" A man came out to the gate,
and I told him that I was sick, and wanted to stay
there for the night.

He kindly told me to go into the house, that he
would put up my horses and feed them.

On entering the door the blazing fire in the fireplace put new life into me. The lady sitting by the
fire looked up, then gave a scream, which brought
her husband on the run. She told him that I had

small-pox. Looking at my face he discovered that it was really covered with fresh small-pox sores. Small-pox was raging in Colorado City, but I never dreamt that I had contracted the dreaded disease.

Now the gentleman told me that I would have to leave, although he hated to drive me out in the cold storm, then raging.

My journey was continued, but on riding about five miles I could stand it no longer. The ponies were tied to a telegraph pole and I laid down with my saddle for a pillow.

At daylight my journey was continued to the next section house, they being ten miles apart, along the railroad.

Before riding up to the section house my face was tied up with silk handkerchiefs, so that the sores couldn't be seen. The section crew had just gone to work, and the man cook gave me a warm meal, which was carried up stairs to be eaten alone, for fear the cook would discover the sores on my face, and run me away. No doubt the cook thought I was an outlaw, trying to keep my face hidden from view. I continued the trick of keeping my face tied up at every section house stopped at enroute. Hard rides were made to reach a doctor in Toyah.

On reaching that town I rode up to Doctor Roberson's office and entered. This prominent railroad doctor pronounced it a case of small-pox, but said the danger had passed, as my pulse was slightly above normal. He gave me some salve to dry up the sores on my face and shoulders, the only places on my body where they had broken out. He also assured me that no one could contract the disease from me, as the fever had gone down.

With my face covered with handkerchiefs, I rode up to the Alvorado Hotel, and was greeted by Miss Beulah, who was out on the front porch. She wanted to know what was the matter with my face, I told her that my mouth was covered with fever blisters.

I hired a boy to care for my horses, and then went to bed, Miss Beulah brought my meals into the room, but I put off eating them until after she left, so that she could not see the sores. The doctor had told me that I would be taken to the pest-house, where there were already several patients, if it was discovered that I had small-pox.

In riding the more than 200 miles from Big Springs, several days had passed.

A few days in bed at the Alvarado Hotel and my journey to El Paso was continued, after bidding Miss Beulah a last farewell. I have never seen this pretty little, tender hearted, girl since, although I have heard of her many times. She is now the wife of a well-to-do Texas cattle-man. I still keep and cherish the leather pocket-book she presented to me on New Years day, 1882. Her name and address being written on the inside.

A ride of 100 miles brought me to the Rio Grande River. That night I camped with a Mexican and his family, they being enroute to El Paso, from Lerado.

Before retiring I moved my ponies to fresh grass, a few hundred yards from camp, "Buckshot" being staked out, and "Croppy" hobbled.

Early next morning I discovered both of my horses gone. I tracked them to the river. On the opposite shore, in Old Mexico, I found moccasin tracks in the sand where the thieves had dismounted to get a drink of water from the river.

Now I returned to camp and hired the Mexican's only saddle pony, his covered wagon being hauled by a yoke of oxen. I agreed to give him $10. a day for the use of the pony.

The tracks of my two ponies were followed west to a range of mountains about thirty-five miles distant. In places I had to ride slowly in order to see the tracks.

It was nearly sun-down when I came in sight of a spring, near which were my ponies. "Buckshot" was staked out to grass and "Croppy" hobbled, just as I had left them the night before.

For a while I hid behind a hill, thinking the thieves would soon show themselves. Finally a shot was heard to the westward, about half a mile distant. I concluded the thieves had gone into the rough mountains to kill game for their supper.

Now I took a drink from the cool spring and headad east, mounted on "Croppy."

It seemed plain to me that two prowling Indians, or Mexicans, afoot had discovered my ponies and rode them into Mexico.

It was daylight when I arrived in camp.

After breakfast I gave the Mexican $10 for the use of his pony, then struck out up the Rio Grande river.

That night I put up with Charlie Wilson, in old Camp Rice, and the next night stopped in the beautiful Mexican town of San Elizario. Here I laid over three days and searched a mountain range in Old Mexico for a herd of cattle which I was told might be stolen stock. I found the herd, but there were no Canadian river cattle in it. No doubt they were stolen stock from the way the three men in charge acted.

I finally reached the adobe town of El Paso—now an up-to-date, beautiful little city—one afternoon.

In riding up the main street a tall man, with steel grey eyes, wearing a city marshall's star called me by name. He was standing on the edge of the sidewalk. I rode over to him and shook his outstretched hand, but I told him that I didn't remember of ever meeting him before.

Now he told of stopping in my camp two days,

in 1878, to reload a lot of rifle and pistol shells.
That he had been run out of Ft. Griffin, Texas,
by the Vigilantes. Then I remembered him, I asked what he did with the herd of sheep he stole
after leaving my camp. This excited him, and he
cautioned me to keep quiet; as some of the pass-
ers-by, on the side-walk, might hear me. He invited me to dismount and take a drink with him,
which I did.

At a table in the rear part of the saloon we had
a long talk, mixed with several drinks of liquor.

This city guardian of the peace wanted to know
how I found out that he had stolen the band of
sheep, I explained that one of my cowboy chums
met him on the Staked Plains driving the sheep
south-westward, with the two Mexican boys as
prisoners. That this chum reported the matter to
me—as he had seen him in my camp, and supposed he was an old friend of mine.

This officer then told me of how he kept the two
boys as prisoners, making them drive the 2000
head of sheep, until they reached the breaks of
the Pecos River in New Mexico, where they were
given their two burros (Jackasses) and told to
"hit the trail" over which they had come.

I said: "Are you sure you didn't kill them, to
prevent them giving the alarm?"

With a laugh he said: "Trust that to me Charlie, for you can bet that I made sure they wouldn't
get help and follow me up."

He then told of driving the sheep to the Pecos
river, where he hired two sheep herders to help
him drive the band to El Paso, where they were
sold for one dollar a head, a total of $2000.

This shows the carelessness of western towns
in the selection of peace officers. I could cite dozens of cases where tough men were appointed
marshals.

These two Mexican boys were in their 'teens,
and had been sent from northern New Mexico into the Texas Panhandle, by their parents, to
guard these sheep.

No doubt their bones were found by the "fool
hoe-men" who afterwards settled that part of the
country. Thus adding another unsolved mystery of
the great Llano Estacado.

Over forty years later, in about the year 1913,
I visited the city of El Paso and tried to find out
the name of this sheep stealing officer; I had forgotten his name.

City detective George Harold assisted me to
find out who wore officers stars in the early' 80s.
Through old-timers we learned that the names of
the two marshals during that period were a Mr.
Studenmeyer and John Sillman.

Mr. Studenmeyer was a tall middle age man,
who was killed in a pistol duel with the Manning
brothers, El Paso saloon men. I satisfied myself
that he was not the sheep thief.

We finally found a Mr. George H. Tucker who

knew John Sillman in Ft. Griffin, Texas. He told of how he had made his escape from the Vigilances there in 1878, that being the same year that the sheep thief stopped in my camp.

Mr. Tucker informed us that John Sillman had a bad record as a killer of men, and a cattle thief, in Ft. Griffin. That he was in partnership, in cattle stealing, with Johnny Larn, whom the Vigilantes shot to death while chained to the floor in jail. He said Sillman killed a man by the name of Cohen, and in some way was mixed up with the killing of seven men, whose bodies were thrown in the river.

John Sillman in 1896 shot and killed the noted man-killer, Wesley Harding, while he was talking to the bar-keeper in one of the saloons in El Paso.

Later, George Scarborough shot and killed Sillman in the alley back of the Wigwam saloon in El Paso.

I later received a letter from John P. Meadows in Tularosa, New Mexico, describing John Sillman. He had worked for him and his partner, Johnny Larn, on their ranch above Ft. Griffin in the early '70s. He described him as being over six feet tall and weighing about 180 pounds, with cold, steel grey eyes. This corresponded with my recollection of him.

I made up my mind without a doubt that John Sillman had stolen the band of sheep, and murdered the two Mexican boys.

Mr. Meadows' letter stated that John Sillman murdered several Mexicans on the Hondo river in Lincoln County, New Mexico.

No doubt when John Sillman murdered Wesley Harding, in cold blood, he thought no jury could be found to convict him for killing the worst man-killer Texas ever produced. But he, himself, was killed before the case came up for trial.

Wesley Harding had the reputation of having killed thirty-one men. No other Texas man had such a high record, with the exception of Bill Longley, who was hanged.

In the middle '70s the state of Texas offered a large reward for "Wess" Harding, dead or alive. This caused him to hide out.

A detective, who needed this reward, opened a store at Cedar Hill, in Gonzales County, near Harding's home. He was later appointed Postmaster for that neighborhood. He kept track of all letters sent, or received, by Harding's wife. Most of these letters came,or went, to a certain town in Florida.

Now, after being a merchant for two years, the detective had business in Florida. Harding was arrested and sent to the Huntsville Penitentiary for twenty-five years, for the killing of a sheriff.

In the penitentiary the officers tried all kinds of schemes, even to whipping him with cato-nine-tails, to make "Wess" work, but he refused to dirty his hands at hard labor.

Now they tried the last resort, by placing him in a vat, to keep the water pumped out, or drown.

After the pump handle was put into "Wess's" hands the water was turned on.

In a moment, when the guard in charge returned, he found the water over Harding's head, and bubbles coming to the surface, showing that no effort had been made to work the pump-handle.

Now Harding was given an easy job as clerk, and served his sentence out.

After gaining his freedom he moved, with his family, to El Paso—there to be murdered by John Sillman.

Detectives George Harold, who assisted me in trying to run down the identity of the officer who stole the herd of sheep, is, no doubt, the slayer of the notorious Sam Bass, although a Mr. Ware got the credit for it.

Mr. Ware has the reputation of killing this outlaw, as he was the leader of the posse who rounded up the gang in Round Rock, Texas.

In this battle Sam Bass and his chum, Barnes were killed, Dad Jackson and Underwood escaped. On the officers side Grimes was killed, and Morris wounded.

Sam Bass was the hero of more young Texas cowboys than any other "bad" man, and the song about him was the most popular. It started out thus:

"Sam Bass was born in Indiana,
It was called his native home.
And at the age of seventeen,
Young Sam began to roam.
He first went out to Texas,
A cowboy for to be;
And a kinder hearted fellow
You'd scarcely ever see."

This song seemed to have a quieting effect on a herd of long-horns during thunder storms. Possibly the sweet, musical tune had something to do with it.

Along the Chisholm trail on a still night these favorite cowboy songs could be heard a long distance, coming from the different herds bedded down for the night.

While laying over in El Paso in 1882, I met John Sykes, a cowboy who drove "up the Chisholm trail" with me in 1876. He could cuss louder and longer than any cowboy in the outfit.

He invited me to his residence to take dinner, and to meet his young wife. She was a handsome, dark haired girl, and had about succeeded in taming her loud-mouth husband.

About thirty years later I met John Sykes in Las Cruces, New Mexico, and found him to be a very tame old man, who had forgotten how to "cuss"—thanks to his wife's training. He now owned an alfalfa farm in the Rio Grande valley, between Las Cruces and El Paso. He has grown children.

I also met Wess Adams, another chum, in El Paso, in 1882. He was the cowboy stabbed by a buffalo hunter in Dodge City, Kansas, in 1877. He now belonged to "Curley Bill's" outlaw gang, and said they were making all kinds of money. He tried to induce me to join the gang. I have never heard of him since.

On the first Monday in April I appeared in Judge Bristol's Court in La Mesilla, three miles from Las Cruces.

John W. Poe and Pat Garrett were there, and so were Mr. and Mrs. George Nesbeth.

Pat Cohglin had employed Col. Rynerson and Thornton to defend him in the court.

Mr. Poe had secured Attorney A. J. Fountain, to assist Prosecuting Attorney Newcomb.

Several years later A. J. Fountain was murdered at the White Sands, between Tularosa and Las Cruces. He was on his way home to Las Cruces, from Lincoln, where he had been attending court. With him in the buggy was a young son, about thirteen years of age.

They stopped for the night in Tularosa. The next morning they started for their sixty mile drive across the White Sands desert.

Late in the afternoon Fountain met the Mexican mail carrier, who advised him to turn back, as he had seen a gang of suspicious characters hiding at the point of White Sands, near a watering place.

This noted lawyer and high degree Mason told the mail carrier that it was of great importance that he be in Las Cruces the next day, so, for that reason, he would have to take a chance on being murdered.

When the mail carrier returned the next day he found Mr. Fountain's buggy by the side of the road, near where he had, on the previous day, seen the suspicious characters.

Underneath the buggy was a pool of blood, and a trail of blood leading away from the buggy -- showing that the murderers had carried the body of Fountain away on one of the horses, attached to the buggy.

When a posse was made up in Las Cruces and Tularosa the bloody trail was followed eastward towards the Guadalupe Mountains.

A camping place was found where a meal had been cooked. Around the camp fire were tracks made by young Fountain, showing that he was still alive. On the ground lay a napkin, with some small silver coins tied up in one corner. These had been presented to the boy by the landlady of the hotel in Tularosa.

Since then no trace has ever been found of Col. Fountain or his son. It still remains one of the mysteries of the White Sands.

Later an ex-convict in Arizona told me that the

boy was killed and thrown into Lost River with his
father's body.

This Lost River would be an ideal place to hide
a crime, as the current would take a dead body
down stream, God knows where. This shallow
stream flows from the White Sands in an easterly
direction, towards the Guadalupe Mountains. It
only shows in one place—a round hole in the
earth, about twenty feet across it. I once laid flat
on my stomach at the edge of this hole and dipped
my had full of water from the stream, flowing
gently a few feet below.

The Mexicans in Tularosa cautioned Sam Coleman and me not to drink this water, as it was
poison. Still we took a chance, without any bad
effects.

It seems that the horse tracks of the murdering
gang led up to a certain cattle ranch. Pat Garrett
and his deputy, John P. Meadows, traced them
there. Later sheriff Garrett and his deputies had
a pitched battle at this ranch house. In the fight
one of Garrett's deputies was shot and killed.

John P. Meadows escaped this battle by being
shot and wounded the day before, when he arrested a Mexican horse thief.

The owner of this cattle ranch and his chums
were finally tried for the murder of A. J. Fountain and his son, but there being no proof that
they were dead, the jury had to bring in a verdict
of not guilty. This wound up the affair.

When the Pat Cohglin case came up for trial that ''Foxy'' gentleman plead guilty to butchering stolen cattle, after being warned by me not to. The Judge fined him $250, along with the costs of the Court. Thus did he dodge the penitentiary gates. Now Mr. Poe brought a $10,000 damage suit against him. I have never learned how that damage case terminated.

Now I was free to ride back to' the LX ranch in the Panhandle of Texas, a distance of about 800 miles.

In bidding Mr. and Mrs. George Nesbeth goodby they told me that they were afraid to travel over the White Sands road, for fear that Pat Cohglin would have them waylaid and murdered, for appearing against him as witnesses. Hence they intended to lay over in Las Cruces a month or two, and slip away when Cohglin got over his angry spell.

They had taken up a homestead above Tularosa, near Blazier's saw mill, on Tularosa River, and intended to make their home there the rest of their lives.

At the point of the White Sands the whole crowd of four were murdered. In a later chapter I will give the facts of this murder, and the trial of the two Mexicans, who confessed to committing the crime for $1,000 of Pat Cohglin's money.

While laying in Las Cruces I contracted a severe case of heart trouble over a pretty little, wealthy, Mexican girl, by the name of Magdalena Ochoa. Therefore I concluded to start a small cattle ranch in this, Dona Ana County, so as to be near the little Miss.

Cowboy Charlie Wall told me of a place that would suit me for a ranch. This being Dog Canyon, the rendezvous of that murdering old renegade Indian Chief, Victoria.

As Charlie Wall had to return to Ft. Stanton he agreed to go with me to Dog Canyon, to examine the water supply.

We started early one morning from the Montezuma Hotel. I threw a farewell kiss at Miss Magdalena, who sat in a window full of pretty flowers and roses, opposite the hotel. As I rode away, mounted on "Croppy," she threw a kiss back at me which reduced the temperature of my heart.

A telegram had been received in Las Cruces that morning, stating that old Victoria and his band of warriors had crossed the Rio Grande river at Colorow—above Las Cruces—during the night, and killed three white men. That they were headed toward Dog Canyon, but this news didn't prevent Wall and me from making the trip. We decided, though, not to camp over night at Dog Canyon.

After passing through San Augustine Pass, twenty-five miles out of Las Cruces, we left the wagon road and turned to the right, cutting across the desert for Dog Canyon, at the foot of the Guadalupe Mountains.

On the second day out of Las Cruces we ate dinner in Dog Canyon. It was a lovely spot, though the stream of sparkling water flowing out of the mountains through the canyon, was small.

I couldn't fully make up my mind to enter a government homestead at this rendezvous of old Victoria.

After making a hurried examination of the land, and water up next to the steep mountains, we rode north to La Luz, a Mexican village, where we put up for the night.

Later a Frenchman took up Dog Canyon as a homestead. He was finally assassinated by unknown parties in the log cabin which he had built.

From La Luz Charlie Wall and I rode north to Tularosa, then turned east, up Tularosa creek.

After crossing over the line of Dona Ana County, into Lincoln County, we came to an alfalfa field to our left, where Charlie Wall had the year previous fought a battle with a crowd of Tularosa Mexicans, who objected to him using water to irrigate this alfalfa field.

When the smoke of battle cleared away four Mexicans lay dead upon the ground, and young Wall had two bullet holes in his body.

Wall had four men helping him irrigate, but they took only a small part in the battle.

To prevent being mobbed, by the angry Tula-

rosa Mexicans Wall and his companions made a
run for Lincoln, to surrender to sheriff Pat Garrett.

The sheriff allowed .them to wear their pistols
and to sleep in the jail.

After continuing our journey up the river
young Wall, who was a modest, truthful fellow,
gave me the full account of "Billy the Kid's"
escape, the year before.

Charlie Wall, not being seriously wounded, did
his loafing in the upstairs room of the Lincoln
Court-house, where "Billy the Kid" was being
guarded.

In La Mesilla the "Kid" had been convicted for
the murder of Sheriff Brady, and Judge Bristol
had sentenced him to be hanged in Lincoln, on
May 13th, 1881.

On the morning of April 28th, while young
Wall was present in the room, Pat Garrett, who
was preparing to leave for White Oaks to have a
scaffold made, remarked to the "Kid's" two
guards: "Watch him carefully, boys, for he has
only a few days to live, and might make a break."

Then Bob Olinger, who had fought against
"Billy the Kid" in the Lincoln County War,
stepped to a closet, against the wall and got his
double-barrel shot-gun.

Looking over towards the "Kid," sitting on a
stool, shackled and handcuffed, Ollinger said:
"There are eighteen buckshot in each barrel and

I reckon the man who gets them will feel it. You
needn't worry, Pat, we will catch him like a
goat.''

With one of his good-natured smiles the ''Kid''
remarked. ''You might be the one to get them
yourself.''

Now Ollinger put the gun back in the closet and
locked the door, putting the key in his pocket.

About five o'clock that evening Bob Ollinger
took Charlie Wall and the other four armed prisoners across the wide street to the hotel for supper, leaving J. W. Bell alone to guard the ''Kid.''

While eating supper Wall says they heard a
shot fired in the court house. They all ran out on
the sidewalk. Ollinger ran towards the courthouse.
In the middle of the street he met the frightened
Mexican jailor, who said: ''Bell has killed the
Kid.''

Now Ollinger quit running and walked to the
court-house. He had to go around to a side stairs,
as there was no up-stairs entrance from the front.

When passing underneath an upstairs window,
which was open, the ''Kid'' called out: ''Hello
Bob!'' Ollinger looked up and saw the ''Kid'',
and the shotgun pointed towards him. Then he
said, loud enough to be heard by Wall and the
other prisoners across the street. ''Yes, he has
killed me, too!''

These words were hardly out of the guard's

mouth when a charge of buck-shot went through
his heart.

A moment later "Billy the Kid" hobbled out
on the small front porch. Around his waist were
two belts of cartridges and two pistols. In his
hands were the shot gun and a Winchester rifle.
These he had secured by kicking open the door to
the gun-closet. Now the "Kid" took aim with the
shot-gun at the dead body of Ollinger and fired,
with the remark: "Take that, you s—of a b—,
you will never follow me with that gun again."
Now he broke the gun in two and threw the pieces
at the corpse.

By this time the sidewalk on the opposite side
of the street was lined with people who had run
out of their houses, on hearing the shots.

Here "Billy the Kid" called to a Mexican,
whom he knew, telling him to throw up a file. This
was done, and the shackle chain was filed apart
in the center, leaving a shackle and piece of chain
on each leg.

Now the "kid" told the Mexican to put a saddle and bridle on the deputy County Clerk's black
pony—which had formerly been owned by the
"Kid"—and bring him out on the street.

This order was carried out.

The "Kid" now, after dancing a jig on the
front porch, went to the side stairs, thence to the
street, where the Mexican was holding the black
pony.

In trying to mount the pony, the "Kid" being encumbered with the heavy load of guns and ammunition, he got loose and ran back to the stable in the courthouse yard.

While waiting for the Mexican to bring the pony back the "Kid" stood in the street holding the rifle ready for action. He would have been an easy target, had it not been that most of the men watching him were sympathizers. Wall says he could have killed him, but he wanted to see him escape.

When the pony was brought back, the "Kid" gave the Mexican his rifle to hold, while he mounted.

Now "Billy the Kid" galloped west, waving his hat and shouting: "Three cheers for Billy the Kid."

When the excitement was over Charlie Wall says he helped the crowd care for the bodies of the two guards. Bell was found at the foot of the stairs with a bullet in his dead body.

The "Kid" told the Mexican friend, who brought him the file and the pony, the secret of his escape. He said Bell was sitting in a chair reading. Then he slipt his left hand out of the handcuffs and made a spring for the guard, striking him on the head with the iron cuff. Instead of Bell pulling his pistol, which was buckled around his waist, he threw both hands up to protect his head from another blow.

Now the "Kid" grabbed the pistol from the holster. Then Bell ran towards the head of the stairs, and as he went to go down, the "Kid" fired. The body went tumbling down the stairs, falling onto the Mexican Jailor, who was sitting at the foot of the stairs. This stampeded the jailor, who ran out on the street where he met Ollinger, telling him that Bell had killed the "Kid."

I am not sure that this Mexican was the jailor. He may have been only an assistant.

After his escape "Billy the Kid" told his friends that he had starved himself, so that the hand-cuff could be slipped over his left hand. The guards supposed he had lost his appetite over the worry of his approaching doom. He said while in bed he used to slip the hand-cuff off to make sure it could be done easily.

In killing Bob Ollinger the "Kid" only gave him a dose of his own kind of medicine. While the Lincoln County war was raging an acquaintance, who was in sympathy with "Billy the Kid's" crowd, stepped up to shake hands with Ollinger, who grabbed the extended right hand with his left. Then with his right hand drew his pistol and shot the fellow to death, he being unable to pull his pistol, as Ollinger was a powerful man, weighing about two hundred pounds.

On arriving in Ft. Stanton Charlie Wall and I separated. I continued on to Lincoln, where I laid over a few days. Pat Garrett and Mr. Poe had already arrived in Lincoln from Las Cruces.

The next day after my arrival the sheriff held an auction to sell "Billy the Kid's" saddle and pistol.

The deputy county clerk and I were the only bidders for the Colts 41 caliber, double-action pistol, which the "Kid" held in his hand at the time of his death.

My last bid was $13, what I thought it was actually worth. The deputy clerk bid $13.50 and got it. I heard that he afterwards sold it for $250 on the strength of it's past history.

While laying over in Lincoln I learned the true account of "Billy the Kid's" death from the three men who had a hand in the affair. These men being Pat Garrett, John W. Poe and "Kip" Mc-Kinnie.

Many stories have been circulated about the under-handed manner in which Garrett murdered the "Kid." Therefore I will here give the true account of it.

About July 1st, 1881 Pat Garrett received a letter from a Mr. Brazil stating that the "Kid" had been seen lately around Ft. Sumner.

The sheriff answered the letter telling Mr. Brazil to meet him at the mouth of the Tayban

Arroyo, on the Pecos river, after dark on July
13th.

Now Garrett took his two deputies, John Poe

PAT GARRETT

and "Kip" McKinnie, and started horse-back, for
the meeting place.

These three officers watched and wa:ted during
the whole night of July 13th, but Mr. Brazil failed
to show up.

On the morning of the 14th they rode up the
Pecos river. When opposite Ft. Sumner the sheriff sent Mr. Poe into that abandoned fort, where
lived many Mexican families, to see if anything
could be learned about the "Kid" having been
there.

Then Garrett and McKinnie rode six miles up
the river to Sunny-side, to keep in hiding until the
arrival of Mr. Poe.

About night John Poe reached Sunny-side and
reported to Garrett that he couldn't find out a
thing of importance about the "Kid." Then the
sheriff said they would ride into Ft. Sumner,
after dark, and see Pete Maxwell, a wealthy sheep
man, and the son of the famous Land Grant Maxwell. The "Kid" was in love with Pete Maxwell's
sister, hence Garrett thinking that Pete might
have seen him hanging around their home.

It was dark when the three officers started on
their six mile journey.

Arriving in Ft. Sumner their horses were tied
in an old orchard. Then they walked into Pete
Maxwell's large, grassy yard. The residence was
a long adobe building fronting south, with a covered porch the full length of the adobe house, Gar-

rett knew the room in which Pete generally slept. The door of this room was open. The sheriff told his two deputies to lie down on the grass, while he went in to talk with Pete.

Now the sheriff lay over on Mr. Maxwell's bed and began questioning him about the ''Kid.'' No one outside of Mr. Garrett was to know what Pete told him.

In the rear of the Maxwell dwelling lived an old Mexican servant, who was a warm friend to the ''Kid.''

Previous to the arrival of the sheriff and his deputies, ''Billy the Kid'' had entered this old servant's adobe cabin. The old man had gone to bed.

''Billy the Kid'' lit the lamp; then pulled off his boots and coat and began reading the news-papers, which had been brought there for his special benefit.

After glancing over the papers the ''Kid'' told the old man to get up and cook him some supper, as he was very hungry, having just walked in from the sheep camp.

The old servant told him that he didn't have any meat in the house. Then the ''Kid'' replied: ''I'll go and see Pete and get some.'' Now he pick-ed up a butcher knife from the table and started, bare-footed and bareheaded.

In walking along the porch to Pete's room,

"Kip" McKinnie saw him coming, but supposed he was one of the servants.

When nearly opposite Pete's room "Kip" raised up and his spur rattled, which attracted the "Kid's" attention. Pulling his pistol he asked in Spanish: "Quien es? Quien es?" (Who's there, who's there?)

Not getting an answer he backed into Pete's room and asked: "Pete, who's out there?"

Maxwell didn't reply. Now the "Kid" saw strange movements in the bed and asked: "Who in the h—l is in here?"

With the pistol raised in his right hand, and the butcher knife in his left, he began backing across the room. Pete whispered in the sheriff's ear. "Thats him Pat."

By this time the "Kid" had backed to the dim moonlight coming through the south window, which shone directly on him, making him an easy target for the sheriff. Bang! went Garrett's Colts pistol, and down went a once mother's darling, shot through the heart.

After the first shot, the sheriff cocked the pistol and it went off accidentally, putting a hole in the ceiling.

The next day Billy Bonney, alias "Billy the Kid", was buried by the side of his chum, Tom O. Phalliard, in the old military cemetery.

A few months later Pat Garrett had the body

dug up to see if the "Kid's" trigger finger had been cut off, but it had not.

A man in the East was showing the front finger of a man, preserved in alcohol. He claimed it was "Billy the Kid's" trigger finger. The newspapers had sensational accounts of it.

Years later when the United States Government employed Will Griffin to remove all dead bodies of soldiers in the Ft. Sumner grave yard, to the National Cemetery in Santa Fe, the graves of "Billy the Kid" and Tom O'Phalliard were the only ones left.

Mr. Griffin, who is still a resident of Santa Fe, says at the time he moved the soldiers bodies there was a board slab marking the "Kid's" grave. Now that old cemetery is an alfalfa field, and those two outlaw graves may have become obliterated.

Before leaving Lincoln, I bade Pat Garrett and John W. Poe goodbye, and never met them again for many years.

Soon after my departure Mr. Poe was elected sheriff of Lincoln County. He afterwards settled in the Pecos Valley, and at this time is a wealthy banker and land owner in the beautiful little city of Roswell, N. M.

On my way home I stopped a few days to visit friends in White Oaks.

I finally arrived at the LX ranch in the Texas Panhandle, after an absence of eight months, and after having ridden horse-back about 3000 miles.

BILLY THE KID

CHAPTER IX

I BECOME MERCHANT IN CALDWELL,
KANSAS. HISTORY OF THE OPENING
OF OKLAHOMA TO SETTLEMENT.

Shortly after my return from New Mexico, Mr.
Hollicot put me in charge of eight hundred fat
steers to be driven slowly to Caldwell, Kansas, on
the southern boundary of that state.

My outfit consisted of a cook, to drive the mess-
wagon, and five riders, with six horses for each
cowboy.

The fourth day of July we were on the north
Staked Plains, and laid over to celebrate the glorious Fourth by resting.

During the forenoon I killed my last buffalo. A
small herd passed our camp and I roped a fat
heifer calf, with the intention of taking it to Caldwell with us, but Lon Chambers and some of the
boys begged that she be butchered for supper.
Their wish was complied with, and we enjoyed
buffalo calf-meat for several days.

The next morning while hunting lost horses I
rode by a bleached buffalo carcas. On one horn
initials had been cut. Through curiosity I dismounted to make an examination. Imagine my
surprise on finding my own initials, C. A. S., and
the year 1877 cut into the horn.

Now the killing of this buffalo bull came back

to my memory, I had forgotten all about the affair.

In the early winter of 1877 I was caught on these plains in a severe blizzard and snow storm. Seeing a lone buffalo bull ahead of me, I made a dash for him, planting a bullet under his hump before he had time to escape.

My pony being hungry and tired, I pulled the bridle off to let him graze, tying the end of the rope to the bull's hind leg.

Now to shield myself from the cold north wind I lay down on the south side of the dead animal, with my head near his horns.

While waiting for the pony to fill up, I cut my initials and the year on one horn.

In order to get these horns to camp I had to drag the head at the end of a rope, as they couldn't be separated from the skull.

Now after the passing of thirty-six years this pair of buffalo horns are hanging on the wall of my bed-room to remind me of the days when millions of buffalo roamed over the Staked Plains.

The bleached carcasses of these wooly beasts became a God-send to the wise "hoe men" who later settled on these plains. Buffalo bones almost became legal-tender, after railroads were built. A wagon load of bones would purchase a good supply of food and clothing.

These new settlers who got the first grab at the pile of bones on the head of Tule Canyon, where

General McKinzie, in 1874, killed the thousands of Comanche ponies, had a snap.

The chances are some human bones were gathered along with the buffalo carcasses, and traded for sugar to make taffy for the little hoe people.

I once found a pile of human bones on the north Staked Plains. They were in a round pile, and bleached white. Many buffalo carcases being near by.

Whoever piled up these bones into a round mound must have known the gentleman who once carried them around with him. On top of the pile was the bleached shoulder blade of a buffalo, on which was carved:

"Here lies the bones of poor Kid Cones,

Whose greatest sin was the love of gin."

We arrived in Caldwell, the "Queen City of the border," about the first of September.

The first man met whom I knew, in this town of over a thousand people, was Henry Brown of "Billy the Kid's" gang, wearing a gold star, as City Marshal. He begged me not to give him away, as he had reformed and intended to lead an upright life.

I foolishly promised to keep the secret to myself. Later he shot and killed an Indian chief, "Spotted Horse," and a cowboy named Boyce, in a cold-blooded manner. It seems he had murder in his heart.

About two years later while still holding the

position of City Marshal, he and his deputy, Ben
Wheeler, and two cowboy friends, rode into Medicine Lodge in broad daylight, without masks, and
held up the only bank in the town, killing the
president, Wiley Payne, and his cashier, George
Jeppert.

In making their get-away, in a rainstorm, headed for the Indian Territory, with a mob of enrag-
ed citizens on their trail, they butted up against
a new barbed wire fence and couldn't get through
it. Now they turned west along the fence and came
to a deep canyon which couldn't be crossed.

Finding themselves hemmed in, with the armed

BARNEY O'CONNOR   TOM DORAN

mob near by, they dismounted and ran down into the canyon afoot, concealing themselves under an overhanging shelf of rock.

The creek kept on rising, inch by inch, finally driving them out of their hiding place, to the open. Many guns from above were leveled at them, and up went their hands.

The leaders of the pursuing party were both cowboy friends of mine, Barney O'Connor and Tom Doran. Mr. O'Connor is now a wealthy cattle man of Garden City, Kansas, and Thomas Doran, with the help of his good-looking, energetic, and jovial wife, is, at this writing, running the Montezuma Hotel in Santa Fe, and the Hotel Doran in the city of Albuquerque, New Mexico.

The four prisoners were taken to Medicine Lodge and their pictures taken, then put into the jail.

After dark a mob was formed and a rush made for the jail. When the door was opened Henry Brown and Ben Wheeler made a break for liberty. Henry Brown received a charge of buckshot, and fell over dead. Ben Wheeler's shirt was set on fire by a shot fired at close range. The blaze from his burning shirt as he ran in the dark made him an easy target for the swift runners behind him. A bullet finally broke his leg.

Now he was carried back and compelled to watch the mob hang his two cowboy companions, then he, too, was strung up on the tree.

Barney O'Connor fell heir to the fine gold mounted Winchester rifle, which the citizens of Caldwell had presented to Henry Brown—their model law-officer.

HENRY BROWN   BEN WHEELER

Soon after arriving in Caldwell our herd of steers were turned loose on the new steer ranch on Turkey Creek, in the Indian Territory, which the LX company had lately established.

Now with my outfit I attended the cattle round-ups in the western part of the Indian Territory, gathering lost LX steers.

It was the last part of November when our work was finished. Then we returned to Caldwell,

where Mr. David T. Beals was awaiting my return. He had purchased a farm on the Indian
Territory line, two miles southeast of Caldwell,
on which to winter the LX cow-ponies.

I was given charge of this farm, and the more
than one hundred head of cow-ponies.

Now I bought some town lots and contracted
the building of a new frame residence. Then I
boarded a train for southern Texas to get Mother.

I went by way of St. Louis to visit my sister
Mrs. George W. Wines, and her family. While in
that city I dropped into the Planter's Hotel to
note the changes since I was bell-boy in that swell
hostelry.

The red-headed bell-boy, Jimmy Byron, with
whom I had the fight, which caused me to throw
up the job as "bell-hop", was now owner of the
news-stand. We buried the hatchet of past hatred
and shook hands.

The former steward was now the proprietor,
and "Old Mike" was still the watchman. The
chief clerk, Cunningham, who had slapped me for
fighting while on duty, was still holding down his
job, but I didn't shake hands with him.

My rail-road journey was continued to the city
of Galveston, in order to visit my Uncle, Nick
White, and his family. Then a Morgan steam-ship
was boarded for what was left of Indianola, since
the great storm of 1875 had washed it away.

My boyhood playmates, Johnny and Jimmie

Williams, were in Indianola with their sail-boat, and they took me to Matagorda.

In Matagorda I laid over a few days visiting my hundreds of friends. Then Jim Keller loaned me a horse and saddle and I rode to Mother on Cashes Creek.

Now I hired Fred Cornelius to take Mother and me over to the Sunset rail-road, fifty miles north.

Mother and I arrived in Caldwell, Kansas, a few days before Christmas. Furniture was bought and a "Home, sweet home" established in my new house.

Now I took charge of the horse ranch, south-east of town, and put in a pleasant winter.

About the first of March I received a letter from Mr. Beals, in Boston, Mass., ordering me to take my crew of cowboys and cow-ponies back to the LX ranch in the Texas Panhandle.

That night after receiving the orders, I attended church with Miss May Beals, a niece of David T. Beals. When church was over she introduced me to her pretty little fifteen year old, black-eyed chum, Mamie Lloyd.

Now I was a sure enough locoed (crazy) cowboy —up to my ears in love.

Six days later, in the Phillips Hotel, in Wellington, the county-seat of Sumner County, Kansas, I was married to Mamie Lloyd—the only daughter of H. Clay Lloyd, of Shelbysville, Illinois. In nailing this pretty little miss to the matrimonial cross

I "shore" won a prize. But the poor girl only lived six years after our marriage, dying in my

MAMIE AND VIOLA

arms in Denver, Colorado. She left a five year
old daughter, Viola, to nearly cry her eyes out
over the loss of a fond mother. Now this once baby
girl, Viola, lives in San Diego, California, and has
an only daughter, twelve years of age, of her own,
her name being Margaret Reid.

Three days after marrying I started for the
Panhandle of Texas in charge of twenty-five cow-

boys, one hundred cow-ponies and six mess wagons.

A journey of eighteen days brought us to the LX ranch.

After a few days rest Mr. Hollicot sent me in charge of a crew to attend round-ups on Red River, and Peas River, in the south-eastern part of the Panhandle.

We arrived at the LX ranch on July 1st with about 3000 head of cattle, which had strayed off during the winter.

Now I started back to Caldwell with 800 fat steers, arriving there about September the first.

Mr. Beals ordered me to take my outfit back to the Panhandle at once and get another herd of fat steers. This I started to do, but after Mr. Beals had taken the train for the east, I suddenly changed my mind. I then turned the outfit over to one of my cowboys, Charlie Sprague, who started for the Panhandle after the other herd.

Then I swore off being a wild and woolly cowboy.

I hated to quit the LX outfit, as Mr. David T. Beals was the best man I had ever worked for. He was an honest, broad-gauge cattle-man.

Many years afterwards I visited him in Kansas City, not knowing that he was almost at the point of death.

On arrival in Kansas City, I dropped into the Union National Bank, of which Mr. Beals was president. The cashier, Mr. Neal, informed me that Mr. Beals was very sick, but would, no doubt, like to see me.

Arriving at the swell residence, 25 Independence Avenue, which, along with the grounds, covered a half city block, I rang the door bell. The young lady servant informed me that the doctor had given orders that no one be allowed to see Mr. Beals.

Writing a note to the sick man on a card, I departed. Before reaching the street Mrs. Beals called me back. She said Mr. Beals would never forgive me if I left without seeing him.

When I reached the sick chamber Mr. Beals sat up, propped against pillows, and gave me a hearty welcome. He said my presence made him feel better.

We "harked back" to the good old cattle days until the five o'clock dinner was ready, then, strange to relate, the old gentleman accompanied me down to the dining room, and ate a hearty meal—the first for a long time.

After Mr. Beals had gone back to bed, his wife showed me through the two rooms full of the most costly wedding presents a cowboy ever laid eyes on. Many of them came from London and Paris.

A few days previous their only daughter, Miss Dora, had married a young Kansas City business man, and they had gone away on their wedding tour.

The only child left was David T. Beals, Jr.—
almost grown to manhood. As a baby he had cost
his father $5000 in hard cash.

When about six weeks old he was kidnapped.
Mr. Beals put advertisements in the city papers
offering a reward of $5,000 for the return of the
baby, and no questions would be asked. That the
money would be in the house ready to be handed
over when the baby was returned.

Two days later, after dark, a rap brought the
cook to the kitchen door. There stood a man and
woman, who told the cook to tell Mr. Beals to
come and get this baby boy.

Putting the infant in it's mother's arms Mr.
Beals got the bag of money and gave it to the
kidnappers, who departed.

After the death of Mr. Beals, young David T.
Beals stepped into his father's shoes, and is now
a successful banker, with a happy family of his
own.

Now I rented a store room on Main Street and
opened a tobacco and cigar store, with confection-
aries as a side issue. I scraped together a few hundred dollars, in order to get started. After that
the sailing was easy, as my credit was unlimited.

Finally I rented an adjoining store room, and
cut an arch-way between the two. In this I opened
up an ice-cream and oyster parlor.

Soon I had five clerks and attendants in my
employ.

About this time there was great excitement over the opening of Oklahoma to settlement. Soldiers were kept on the border of the Indian Territory to keep the ''Oklahoma boomers'' out of the ''promised land.''

Still the ''boomers'' would slip by the soldiers in the night. Many were arrested and jailed in Wichita.

Capt. D. L. Payne was at the head of the movement, and Capt. Couch was second in command.

While the soldiers were napping several hundred ''Oklahoma boomers'' stole a march on them in the night. The next day the ''Oklahoma War Chief,'' with Samuel Croker as editor in Chief, was issued in it's new home, a frame shack hauled over the line from Kansas.

This, the first newspaper ever published in Oklahoma, was issued several miles south of the line, on Chikaskia Creek, south-east of Hunnewell, Kansas.

With the large crowd gathered together, at the ''Oklahoma War Chief's'' new home, a photograph was taken.

Of course the United States Soldiers, stationed at Caldwell, finally woke up and captured the ''Oklahoma War Chief'' and it's editor, burning the shack, and marching the big and little ''boomers'' back over the line into Kansas.

On one of these raids into Oklahoma, Capt. D. L. Payne built a log house, on the Canadian River,

"OKLAHOMA WAR CHIEF"

and established a home. But his "home, sweet home" only lasted until the soldiers could reach him. His photograph and the log house was taken before his arrest.

Big-hearted Capt. D. L. Payne, the hero of all "boomers," died before Oklahoma was opened to settlement. He dropped dead while eating a meal at a hotel in Wellington, Kansas.

Now Capt. Bill Couch stepped into Capt. Paynes shoes, and became the "big chief" of the "Oklahoma boomers."

Owing to the fact that their bitter enemies, the U. S. Soldiers and the Indian Territory cattlemen, made Caldwell their headquarters, the "boomers" left, and established headquarters in Arkansas City, Kansas, thirty-five miles east.

This didn't suit the citizens and business men of Caldwell, so one night we held a mass-meeting to remedy the matter.

It was Saturday night. A collection of $600 in cash was taken up, and a Mr. Miller and I were appointed a committee to visit Arkansas City, on the quiet, and induce the "boomers" to re-establish headquarters in Caldwell.

Bright and early Sunday morning Mr. Miller and I started east in a buggy, drawn by a spirited pair of sorrels.

We arrived in the "boomer's" camp, in the outskirts of Arkansas City, in time to eat dinner with Capt. Couch, his secretary, John A. Blackburn,

CAPT. D. L. PAYNE

and Samuel Crocker, who had brought the "Oklahoma War Chief" back to life.

Mr. Miller and I explained our business, and showed the $600 collected the night before. And we promised that more money would be produced to feed the little hungry "boomers" when needed.

There were many poverty-stricken "boomers" with large families, who needed free grub and clothing.

After dinner Capt. Couch called the people together, and in a speech, told them of our mission.

A vote was taken, and carried, to re-establish headquarters in Caldwell.

Now Mr. Miller and I paid over the $600, and returned home.

Early the next morning the road along the Kansas border was lined with the 600 big and little "boomers," some afoot and others in vehicles.

Arkansas City was angry when she awoke to the fact that Caldwell had stolen a march on her, while she slept.

Soon after this I became the "Oklahoma border" cigar King. A lot of 100,000 cigars were ordered from an eastern factory, put up in my own special brand, called "The Oklahoma Boomer." They sold like hot cakes.

In order to catch the cowboy trade, coming to town from the Indian Territory, I had a large oil-painting made, which was locked with iron chains to the overhead frame work of the iron bridge across Bluff Creek.

The painting showed a mounted cowboy with a long-horn steer at the end of his rope. Over this was my "Oklahoma Boomer" cigar advertisement.

Cowboys leaving town drunk were in the habit of shooting this nice oil painting full of holes. The last time I saw it about twenty years later, it was riddled with bullet holes.

On the first day of May, 1885, Caldwell put on her Sunday Clothes and held a grand cowboy tournament at the fair grounds. Cowboys and cattlemen from all over the Indian Territory were there to witness the sport.

One of the games was catching small rings with a long pole, while the pony was running his best, the prize being a fine ladies gold ring.

I had promised my sixteen year old wife that she would wear the ring, and the promise was fulfilled, as I won against the dozens of competitors.

In the steer-roping match I won a fine silver cup, hog-tying the steer in forty-four seconds. The first time I threw him he jumped to his feet, after I had dismounted. Then springing back in the saddle, I had to throw him again. Even with all this lost time the silver cup was awarded to me, and it is kept as a relic of by-gone days.

My mount was a "cracker-jack," black pony

borrowed from Cattle King John Blair, now an automobile dealer of Wichita, Kansas.

While running my store I wore high-heel cowboy boots, and red silk sash around my waist.

Finally my silk sash disappeared, and another couldn't be purchased in this northern country. There was nothing to do but wear suspenders to keep my pants up, and this almost broke my heart.

Several months later "Shanghai" Pierce stopped off in Caldwell, and took dinner with us.

While at the dinner table Mr. Pierce expressed surprise at me wearing suspenders, instead of a silk sash. Here Mamie, my girl wife, confessed that she had burnt my silk sash, so that I would have to wear suspenders. Of course I forgave her before she died.

The "Oklahoma boomers" increased in numbers, and kept the soldiers busy running them out of the milk and honey land. Finally Congress passed a bill opening Oklahoma to settlement.

In the spring of 1889, when the grand rush was made for free homes in Oklahoma, by the thousands of "boomers," cattle men and cow-boys, it became the greatest human stampede ever pulled off.

The rush was made from all sides, but the greatest crowd was on the Kansas border, where a large force of U. S. Soldiers held the crowds back until the word was given to "go."

Now a new state was born, though she was kept

in baby "Panties" for several years; then allowed to wear Statehood clothing, adding another
star to our glorious American Flag.

On the first anniversary of the opening of Oklahoma, in the spring of 1890, I helped celebrate
the day in the swift little city of El Reno, built
on the old Chisholm cattle trail, a few miles below Ft. Reno, on the North Canadian River.

In the short period of one year many other embryo cities sprang up, on, or near the Chisholm
trail, among them being Hennessey, Enid and
Kingfisher. A year or two later, Chickasha, now
one of the leading cities of Oklahoma, sprang into
existence on the Washita River.

The next day after the anniversary celebration,
in El Reno, I visited Oklahoma City—now the
capital, and largest city in the state.

Here I found a city of tents and shacks scattered all over creation.

My friend, Samuel Crocker, editor of the "Oklahoma War Chief," was found living on his
homestead at the edge of town. He had already
sold 80 acres of his 160 acre tract, as city lots.

Poor Capt. Couch, of the original "Oklahoma
boomers," had secured a farm near Oklahoma
City, but it cost him his life, as he was shot and
killed in a dispute over the claim.

I found my friend, John A. Blackburn, secretary of the original "boomers," had been elected county clerk in Oklahoma City.

Many fortunes were made in Oklahoma City real estate, and in a few years costly business blocks were erected. The Colcord Building was the pride of the city in later years. It was built by Col. Colcord who, in the early cattle days, owned the stage line south of Caldwell. The opening of Oklahoma had made him wealthy, placing him on "easy street," along with hundreds of other old-timers who had endured hardships along the Kansas and Indian Territory border.

Two years and a half as a successful business man swelled my head, so that I thought I was a natural born financier. Caldwell became too small for a man of my caliber. Therefore, the store and other interests were sold, and in the early spring of 1886, I moved to the city of Chicago, a place more fitting for the expansion of my financial abilities.

A few months in that great city convinced me that the proper place for me to shine was in the saddle. I had butted into men with genius financial abilities, and in short order, they almost put me on the "Bum."

CHAPTER X.

A VISIT TO MY OLD STAMPING GROUND IN SOUTHERN TEXAS.

THE TRUE HISTORY OF THE STARTING, AND NAMING OF THE OLD CHIS-HOLM CATTLE TRAIL

During the spring of 1886, while I was living in the city of Chicago, the great Haymarket riot took place. A bomb thrown into a squad of policemen killed and wounded sixty officers

The excitement over the matter made me think that I might be a natural born detective instead of a financier. Hence I applied for a position with Pinkerton's National Detective Agency, and was accepted. They had just established a branch agency in Denver, Colorado, and needed a cowboy detective out there to work on the western cattle ranges, and among outlaws.

The first work assigned to me in Chicago was on the haymarket Anarchist case. I continued on it until the leaders; Ling, Parsons, Engel, Fisher, Schwab, Fielding and Neebe were convicted, four being hanged, and two sent to the penitentiary. Ling blew his head off with a bomb, in the jail, before the time for execution.

During the fall I departed for Denver, Colorado, where, for twenty-two long years I made my headquarters, and continued in the employ of the Pinkerton Agency.

Naturally these twenty-two years proved a great schooling for a once wild and woolly cowboy. Many times my life was saved by a mere hairs-breadth, and I had the opportunity of seeing parts of the United States, Old Mexico, British Columbia and the coast country of Alaska.

During eight months of this time I was in the saddle as a "cowboy-outlaw" in the mountains of Kentucky and Virginia.

One of my operations in the saddle as a "cowboy outlaw," under assumed names, as a member of the "Wild Bunch" of "bad" men, lasted for four years, until one of the worst gangs of murderers, train and bank robbers, were broken up. This operation took me into all the western states and Old Mexico, also into Tennessee and Arkansas.

My work through the Bad Lands of South Dakota placed me among a new kind of "fool hoemen." The new settlers of Texas and Oklahoma had it easy, compared with these Bad Land settlers.

Many times during the winter months I have put up for the night in one of the sod houses called "home sweet home" by these hardy "hoe-men," when it was impossible to get near the stove, or fire-place, on account of the shivering children huddled around the fire to keep warm.

"HOME SWEET HOME" OF A HOE-MAN IN THE BAD LANDS
OF SOUTH DAKOTA

In many cases wood or coal had to be hauled
thirty to fifty miles, so you can imagine the neces-
sity for small fires, even though the thermome-
ter was hovering below the zero mark Also in
some cases water had to be hauled long distances.

Those same conditions existed in parts of
North Dakota, Montana, Wyoming and Nebraska.

By rights Uncle Sam should have furnished
free fuel and water to go with the free land given
to these ''fool-hoe-men'' of the north.

Nearly a year of my time was spent in the saddle in the Horse Heaven country of eastern Ore-
gon, where I saw more fine range horses than I
had ever seen before. It should have been named
Cowboy Heaven, as good horses means Heaven to
a cowboy.

Here, even in mid-winter, these thousands of
wild horses could fill up on green bunch grass by
pawing the snow away. They were kept seal fat
the year 'round. One man in Crook County, a Mr.
Brown, had 5000 horses on his range and they
were all well-bred stock.

During the early '90s I concluded to take another matrimonial chance. This time is was a pretty
blue-eyed girl, Miss Lillie Thomas, of Denver. We
lived together long enough to have one son. Lee
Roy, who at this writing, has discarded his soldiers uniform, which he put on to help lick that
Kaiser Wilhelm bunch. He is now back in a South-

ern California bank, holding down an official position.

Lillie and I agreed to disagree because she wanted to live in Los Angeles, California, while I insisted on making the Rocky Mountains my home.

Although the matrimonial knot was severed, we still remain good friends, and correspond with each other. She often sends me nice fruits from her California orchard.

In the fall of 1887, one year after landing in Denver, I took part in a roping and riding match which took place at the Riverside Park. It was the first cowboy tournament ever pulled off in Denver, and the whole city turned out to see it.

I had just returned from a cowboy operation in western Colorado, and had sold my saddle. Hence I had to hire an old Texas saddle for the tournament. I also hired a small white cow-pony for the occasion.

Here is what the two leading daily papers, the Republican, and the Rocky Mountain News said about me the next morning. I was under the assumed name of ''Dull Knife,'' as I didn't want the public to know who I was:

''When Dull Knife rode in armed with pearl-handled pistol and knife, a gold embroidered Mexican sombrero on his head, and mounted on a quick-reined white pony, he was such a perfect and graceful type of a Texas cowboy that the audience gave one spontaneous Ah-h-a of admiration. The little white pony was a daisy and ran up on Dull Knife's broncho easy. Dull Knife was the only man this day to rope and throw his broncho on horseback. But the rope had fouled in the broncho's mane, and it was choking to death, so Dull Knife cut the rope, mercifully freed the broncho and lost his time to ride. Dull Knife essayed roping and tying but luck was against him. The horn of his light Mexican saddle broke off close to the fork. Regaining his rope he tied it in the forks of his saddle, and tried it again, but his beautiful little cut horse was too light to hold the big burley steer which dragged it all over the corral, so Dull Knife, chafing with chagrin, had to give in to hard luck and call it a draw.''

The other daily paper gave this account:

''None knew who the next man was who rode out on a white pony. They called him Dull Knife, and he was from Meeker. That was all the information obtainable. But Dull Knife was a daisy. With white sombrero, Mexican saddle, leather chaparejos, flaming red handkerchief, belt and pearl handled revolver and knife, he was all that the eastern imagination of the typical cowboy could picture. A bay was pointed out to him and away they flew. It didn't take that cunning bay broncho more than a minute to find out that he was wanted. With all the natural cussedness of his breed it didn't take him more than a second to determine that he would fool somebody. Dashing

here and there, with flashing eyes and streaming
mane and tail, the animal was a pretty picture.
The white pony was too cunning for him though,
and soon put his rider in a position where the
rope could be thrown and the arched neck caught
in the running loop. The captive was thrown,
then Dull Knife made a skillful move. He cut the
rope loose and held the struggling animal by the
nose. But while he was subduing the horse, the
man had gotten too far away from his saddle and
couldn't get back to it. The judges at length called
time and the pretty bay was free.

"Dull Knife and E. A. Shaeffer next stretched
a steer in quick time."

The reason I lost my chance to ride this wild
broncho was because, in running from my mount
to the fallen broncho, the hackamore and leather
blind fell to the ground, away from my reach, and
according to the rules, no one was allowed to hand
them to me. They had been tucked under my pistol
belt. There I sat on the broncho's neck, holding
him down by the nose, with the hackamore and
blind almost within reach. There was nothing to
do but free the animal.

Had it not been for this mishap, I feel confident
that I would have won the large prize. Still, the
managers of the tournament presented me with a
special prize of fifteen dollars, for "skillful cowboy work."

In the early fall of 1907, after a twenty-two

DENVER EXPOSITION.

$165.00 (Fifteen [?] & 100 Dollars)

Denver, Oct. 15th 1887.

Pay to the order of Dull Knife

—— Premium on

Skillful Cowmanes at
Cowboys Tournament

GEO. L. GOULDING,
Supt. Live Stock Department.

To THOS. E. POOLE, Treas.

By W. White .... ENTRY CLERK.

CHECK FOR SKILLFUL COWBOY WORK

years eventful life as a cowboy detective, I resign-
ed from Pinkerton's National Detective Agency,
and moved onto my Sunny Slope ranch in the outskirts of the capital city of Santa Fe, New Mexico.
Many years before, I had selected Santa Fe as a
home, owing to its fine summer climate, and the
broad-gauge, brotherly spirit of its citizens.

Even though I had two pet saddle horses to
ride, I found this "simple life" not strenuous
enough. Therefore I accepted a detective operation at eight dollars a day and all expenses, which
came to me through the Wm. J. Burns Detective
Agency of Chicago, as they had no suitable detective for the work, which was to be done in the
state of Nevada.

I was absent on this operation, which proved a
success to the clients, nearly a year, and made
some easy money.

In 1910 the Wm. J. Burns Detective Agency, of
Chicago, employed me on another operation, in
Arizona, to decide who had robbed a bank there.
As I decided that "Kid Curry" was the robber, I
will here give a sketch of his life, and the daring
robbery in Arizona.

Among the latter-day "bad" men, Harvey Logan, alias "Kid Curry" had no equal as a dare
devil.

He was brought up in Dodson, Missouri, above
Kansas City, and at an early age drifted to Texas
and Colorado to become a cowboy.

In 1884 he got into a "jack-pot" in Pueblo, Colorado, and had to hit the high places to escape the officers of the law, several bullets striking the buggy in which he made his getaway.

He finally landed in the Judith Basin, Montana, and with his brothers, Johnny and Loney, started in the cattle and horse business, with no capital but branding irons and lassos.

A few years later, in a saloon fight, he killed old Pike Landusky, in the Little Rockies of northern Montana.

Now he became an outlaw right. In Nebraska he held up a bank, and was shot through the wrist while making his get-away. This wound branded him for life. Had it not been for his wound, some of his friends might think that his body now lies in a train-robber's grave, on Grand River in Colorado.

A train was held up, and one of the robbers killed; his body being identified by a man who was supposed to know, as that of "Kid Curry." Later the body was dug up to see if there was a wound in the wrist, but there was not.

At the time of this train hold-up, the newspapers were full of the account of "Kid Curry's" connection with it, and of his death. Soon after, one of "Kid Curry's" chums, Jim Furgerson, who lived near the scene of the robbery, wrote me, under my assumed name of Harry Blevins to Silver City, New Mexico, telling of the robbery,

and of how the officers thought the dead robber
was "Kid Curry." The letter stated: "The man
who was killed, stopped with me up to the time the
train was held up, and I know he was not "Kid
Curry."

This letter should be on file in Wm. J. Burns'
Agency, in Los Angeles, California, as I sent it to
the superintendent there, as proof that the man
buried on Grand River was not "Kid Curry."

Jim Furgerson, who wrote me this letter, was
an ex-convict outlaw, and was in Nebraska when
"Kid Curry" was shot in the wrist.

He had no reason to write me a falsehood, as
he supposed I was an outlaw. In about the year
1910, the Gila Valley Bank, in Morencia, Arizona,
was held up by a lone robber.

Morencia is a mining camp of about 5,000 population. It is situated in a basin, with no way to get
in or out on horseback, except down the canyon
past the machine-shop, where 250 men were employed.

About 10 A. M. the lone robber tied his horse
in front of the hotel and bank; the bank being on
the lower floor and the hotel upstairs.

Carrying a double canvas bag in his hand, the
robber entered the bank. He then deliberately
pulled down the shade, or curtain, to the glass
front door which he locked. Now he threw his
Colt's pistol down on the cashier and bookkeeper,

the only occupants of the bank. Of course their hands went up in the air.

On reaching the inside of the private enclosure, the bandit asked the cashier to dump his loose change into the canvas bag. This netted only about $1,500.

Now the cashier was led into the outer vault, the door of which was open. In one corner lay a pile of silver dollars, in sacks. The cashier swore by all that was holy, that he couldn't open the inside vault, where the bulk of the money was kept, as no one but the manager of the company store knew the combination. Of course this was a falsehood but the bandit didn't know it.

The holdup man then held open his double-geared sack and told the cashier to put in some of the silver, which he did, putting in nine hundred dollars in all.

Now the robber called the bookkeeper and told him and the cashier to get into the vault, so he could lock them up. They both pleaded with him not to shut them in the steel vault, as they would smother before any one could find and release them.

A tender spot was touched in the bandit's heart. He asked if they would keep still and not give the alarm until after he mounted his pony. They promised by the Virgin Mary and all the saints in Heaven.

Now the robber shouldered his heavy sack and

started for his mount, tied to the rack about one hundred yards distant. He had only got half way to the horse when the cashier and bookkeeper came out on the porch and cut down on him with a double-barrel shotgun and a pistol. The charge of shot hit the ground near his feet. He then coolly sat the sack down, and pulling his pistol, made the two bankers hide out. Bullets from his pistol hit the walls close to them.

Now he shouldered the sack and got to his horse, when an insurance agent ran out on the porch and began shooting with a small twenty-two caliber pocket pistol. No attention was paid to this until after he had put the sack of money over the saddle horn. Then he got his Winchester rifle from the saddle scabbard, and took one shot at the man with the toy pistol. The bullet from his high power rifle buried itself in a pillar of the porch, a few inches above the man's head. Of course the fellow made himself scarce after this shot.

By this time the street in front of the company store was full of laborers, attracted by the shooting; also the road in front of the machine-shop, over which the robber had to go, was full of men.

Mounting his horse, and holding the rifle in his right hand, he went flying down the steep hill. On reaching the machine-shop, where the hundred or more men were lined along the road, he checked his mount up into a trot and turned the barrel of the rifle toward the crowd. This caused a scattering; some crawling away on their hands and knees.

The bandit laughed loud enough to be heard by some of these men, who told me about it a week or so later.

Now the robber put spurs to his mount and turned to the west, over a side road. He could see the two deputy sheriffs—who had run into the store to get rifles—coming on his trail as fast as their horses could run.

On reaching the top of a ridge the bandit quit the road and turned down a gulch.

When the officers came in sight the robber was several hundred yards down the gulch. Soon he disappeared. He had jumped his mount over a precipice, twelve feet high, into a sandy arroyo.

On reaching the place the officers could see the horse's tracks in the sand, going down the bed of the gulch.

These officers were old time cowboys, but they didn't have the nerve to jump over the cliff—and I couldn't blame them after seeing the place, at which time the robber's horse tracks still showed in the sand.

The distance of the first tracks from the cliff showed that the horse was running when he went over.

There was nothing for the officers to do but to go down the ridge quite a distance, to the first place where they could enter the gulch. They found the robbers tracks and followed them 'till they were lost on a stony flat. They were then headed north-east toward Alma, New Mexico, the outlaws' paradise.

When I arrived on the scene the two officers rode over the ground and showed me the robber's trail.

I spent a week or two investigating this robbery and came to the conclusion that the hold-up man was "Kid Curry." Out in the hills I found some men who had seen him before the robbery—and their descriptions tallied with that of "Kid Curry."

The day before the robbery two Mexicans, returning to their camp for dinner, saw this bandit asleep on his saddle, with his horse grazing at the end of a rope near by. They called to him, and he jumped up holding a Winchester rifle ready for action. They invited him to their camp for dinner He replied that he wasn't hungry.

In my investigations I found out that just before this robbery "Kid Curry's" old pal, Bob McGinnis, who had been pardoned from the penitentiary, had sold his saloon in Alma and dropped out of sight.

Another old pal, "Butch Cassaday," who had formerly run a saloon in Alma for four years, under the name of Jim Lowe, was seen with McGinnis not long before the hold-up.

No doubt the bandit selected his route, knowing that very few law officers would risk their necks in following him over that cliff.

"Kid Curry" knew every foot of this whole country, as he had been a cowboy along the line of New Mexico and Arizona, under the name of Tom Capehart.

Several years previous, Capehart had shot and killed Geo. Scarborough, the man who did a noble deed when he killed John Sillman, the murderer of Wesley Harding in El Paso, Texas.

The killing of Scarborough took place just before the writer joined "Kid Curry's" wild bunch, who operated from the hole-in-the-wall, in Wyoming, and the Little Rockies in Montana, to Alma, New Mexico, and the northern border ot old Mexico.

Walter Birchfield, a cattle man of Deming, New Mexico, was with Scarborough when he was killed. The boys used to tell in my presenec of how Birchfields life was spared, as they liked him on account of his many acts of kindness toward Capehart, when he was a cowboy near Deming.

Only his warmest friends know what became of "Kid Curry" after he escaped from the sheriff at Knoxville, Tennessee.

This sheriff was paid $8000 to let "Kid Curry" escape, after his conviction for life, and the chances are that Jim T——, who owned a horse ranch in partsership with "Kid Curry," near Landusky,

Montana, furnished this money, as he was in
Knoxville at the time.

The Knoxville sheriff was arrested and thrown
in jail for accepting this bribe.

"KID CURRY"

The crime for which "Kid Curry" was convicted was passing unsigned United States cur-
rency, secured in a Great Northern train hold-up.
But the cause of his arrest was the shooting of
two police-officers, in Knoxville.

He was playing pool with a stranger when an
argument arose over the game. "Kid Curry"
knocked the stranger down with his cue. This
caused the proprietor of the hall to whistle for
the police. "Kid Curry" then ran out of the door,

just as two officers were entering. They demanded his arrest. He drew his pistol and shot both
down—though both finally recovered from the
wounds. One of these officers used his club on
"Kid Curry's" head before he fell.

Now the cowboy "bad man" ran   for   the
swamps. Bloodhounds were put on his trail. He
was found leaning against a tree, almost uncon-
scious from the blow on the head. When told to
throw up his hands, by the officers who followed
the hounds, he paid no attention, although wide
awake.

This was the story told to me in Knoxville, later. There I made the acquaintance of one of the
two wounded policemen.

Jim T——, who owned about 500 head of fine
range horses in partnership with the "Kid," told
me that he was the cause of "Kid Curry" becoming an outlaw, therefore he would remain his
friend until death.

He said that after the rough and tumble fight in
the saloon, in the town of Landusky, Mont., (the
fight starting over Pike Landusky calling "Kid
Curry" a nigger, on account of his very dark skin
and hair." "The Kid" walked up to where he
(Jim T—,) was sitting on the saloon bar, wiping
the blood from his face. Then Jim T— says he remarked: "If I were you I would kill the old devil."

He said he had no idea that the "Kid" would take his words seriously.

Now "Kid Curry" pulled out his pistol and shot Pike Landusky dead—thus starting on the down-grade as one of the most daring robbers and murderers of the age.

He killed many men, one of them being a Mr. Winters, who, in self defense, shot and killed his brother, Johnny Logan. His other brother, Loney Logan, was shot and killed by law officers in trying to effect his capture, while he was in hiding at his aunt's (Mrs. Lee) house near Dodson, Missouri. With a pistol in his hand he ran out of the house and was shot through the head by Ben Kimble.

In 1912 I ate Christmas dinner in Santa Fe, New Mexico, then put my two pet saddle horses, Rowdy and Pat in a box car and started them south, ahead of me. In the same car was my large Russian wolf-hound dog. Eat 'Em up Jake, who could whip his weight in wild cats and not half try. My saddle, pack outfit, and bedding were in the same car.

On the morning after Christmas I boarded a passenger train and overtook the horse car in Belen—where the stock were watered and fed, then sent on to Amarillo, Texas.

I was starting out for the Gulf coast of Texas to visit my boyhood stamping ground, and in the spring to ride up the old Chisholm cattle trail to it's northern end, Abilene, Kansas, a distance of about 1200 miles. I was anxious to see how much of this old trail had escaped being torn to pieces with plows and hoes.

In the little city of Amarillo, built near the Amarillo lake, where I had in 1877, seen a million buffalo in one black mass, I laid over a day and night to visit former cowboy friends. One of these friends owned a butcher shop, in which hung a dressed buffalo bull, which he had purchased from Charlie Goodnight, to be sold on New Years Eve, at one dollar a pound.

From this buffalo bull a hump loin was cut and presented to me as a treat.

On leaving Amarillo the passenger conductor and his brakeman put the hump loin on ice, then telegraphed ahead to the manager of the Harvey House in Sweetwater, which was the end of the division, on the A. T. & S. F. Ry. to prepare us a fine midnight supper, all but the meat, which we would furnish.

The brakeman of this train, Mr. F. A. Dumek, had been a buffalo hunter during the early '70s in Nebraska and Dakota. I asked him how many buffalos he had seen at one time. He felt sure he had seen 10,000,000 head in one body as far as the eyes could reach.

Even though he stretched the truth by 9,000,-000 head, that would leave a good sized herd, equal to the band seen by me at Amarillo lake.

We arrived in Sweetwater City at midnight.
The manager of the Harvey House was waiting
for us, to fill up on buffalo hump. The supper was
fine, this being my last taste of buffalo meat.

On New Years day my ponies were unloaded in
Bay City, the up-to-date county seat of Matagorda
County. Here at this very spot I had helped round
up wild four year old mavericks in 1867. Little did
I dream then that a young city would spring up
on Bay Prairie, surrounded by prosperous farmers.

From Bay City, mounted on my sorrel stallion,
Rowdy, with Pat carrying the pack on his back, I
started for the little city of Palacios, built on
Hamiltons Point, the place where I spent that
dreadful night in the great storm of 1875.

In Palacios I met old friends by the hundreds.
Here lived my boyhood chum Billy Williams, and
his wife, who, as Miss Martha Franz, was once the
belle of Matagorda County. And here also lived
my former cowboy chum, Nolan Keller, and the
once little boy, Johnny Pierce, whom I escorted
to and from school at the old Rancho Grande headquarters, while I was on crutches. Now I find him
a wealthy banker, with Nolan Keller's pretty
black-eyed daughter as his wife.

My old millionaire employer, John E. Pierce,
heard that I was in the country and came down
from Blessing—a town built with his money—to
take me home with him. Of course I went, and

put in a whole week of high living at his fine new hotel in Blessing.

While his guest, Mr. Pierce drove me in his buggy, drawn by a spirited team of bays, to see the old Rancho Grande headquarters. On the way there, while driving through the timber, Eat 'Em Up Jake showed his skill as a fighter.

We were nearing a large white frame house by the side of the road. Mr. Pierce stopped the team and told me to put Eat 'Em Up Jake in the buggy, as, at this house there was a vicious brute which had killed many dogs.

I laughed at the idea of him killing my dog, so I told Mr. Pierce to drive on, and just watch Jake take care of himself.

When opposite the house there came a large black dog on the run, with a little yellow fice at his heels. Jake was trotting along ahead of us. The big brute sprang onto his back and mashed him to the ground. While the fight was raging, the fice kept nipping Jake on the hind legs. He quit the black dog long enough to toss the little fice up into the air the height of our buggy top. When he hit the ground he flew for home yelping. The big dog soon followed suit, with tail between his legs. Nearly every jump he made Jake would grab him by the hind quarters and give him a complete somersault. They were soon out of sight, in the rear of the dwelling. What happened there we never knew. But Eat 'Em Up Jake came back to

the buggy covered with blood, but not his own
blood, as he came out of the fight without a
scratch.

Mr. Pierce was so tickled and joyful over this
dog-killing brute finally meeting his match, that
he acted like a school boy. He had to tell all his
friends in Blessing about the great fight.

We finally reached the old Rancho Grande
headquarters, which had changed since my last
visit to the place.

We then drove to the old church house and
grave-yard to see "Shanghai" Pierce's $10,000
statue, made of bronze, and erected before his
death. It stood forty feet high, and was as natural as life. In imagination I could hear "Shanghai's" voice, which could be heard nearly half a
mile, even when he tried to whisper.

After my week's visit with Mr. Pierce I went
to the town of Midfield to eat free grub for several days with cattleman Fred Cornelius, and his
pleasant family. While there I rode with him
over his range to see the long-horn cattle wearing
the brand T.5. connected, which I sold to him forty
years previous.

Of course I had to visit my old boyhood partner, Horace Yeamans, who lived in College-Port
—a town built across the bay from Palacios.
Mounted on my saddle horses he and I rode thru
the streets of these would-be cities and marveled
at the great changes which had taken place in for-

ty years, since we used to brand mavericks and skin cattle on this once wild prairie land.

Now my horses were left in care of that old-time prince of cowboys, Nolan Keller, who is now weathly, and Eat 'Em Up Jake and I then boarded a train for the west, to visit Port Lavaca, Corpus Christi and other towns along the coast.

One of the objects of this trip was to dig up the hidden secret of how the old Chisholm cattle trail derived its name.

Most cattlemen and cowboys think it was named after the Pecos River Cattle King, John Chisum. But I felt sure it was not, as the names are spelt different, and John Chisum never drove cattle up that trail to Kansas.

In Port Lavaca I found a banker, W. C. Noble, who drove "up the Chisholm trail" eight times, and still he couldn't tell how the trail got it's name. But he felt sure that if I would go and see Col. Chisholm, who had a ranch on the Nueces River, the secret would be solved.

A train took me to a small station, where a team and buggy were hired for the trip.

I found Col. Chisholm to be a giant in size, with snow white hair. He almost burst his sides laughing at the idea of the trail being named after him. He said he had never driven anything in his life but a yoke of oxen.

On the trip I talked with hundreds of old trail

drivers, but none could tell me the secret, so I re-turned to Palacios.

Shortly after my return, Billy Williams, my boyhood chum, and I started across country, mounted on my saddle horses, for the town of Matagorda, twenty-five miles distant.

We rode in sight of a round mott or bunch of timber, which brought back memories of my fool cowboy days on this, then, wild prairie.

This mott of timber stood on a 2200 acre tract of land which the owner, in 1873, offered to sell for ten cents an acre. I had nearly cash enough to buy it, and Mr. Jonathan Pierce offered to loan me the balance, without interest. He argued that it would make me rich if I would buy and hang onto it, until the country settled up.

The skin was scratched off my scalp trying to make up my mind whether to buy it or not, I finally decided that it never would be worth over one dollar an acre, so turned the deal down, and Mr. Pierce bought the tract at ten cents an acre.

While visiting Mr. Pierce in Blessing, he told me of how he had sold some of this land, recently, at $150 an acre. The lowest price received being $60 an acre after being cut into small tracts.

This shows how some men are born to look into the future, while others can't see further than the end of their noses. I belong in the latter class, and now felt like hiring a cheap man to kick me good and hard.

In Matagorda "Billy" and I made our home
. with Mr. Baltis Ryman and his family, the chief
head cook of this swell home being Mrs. Ryman,
"Billys" sister.

A week was spent shaking hands, and "hark-
ing back," with old friends and their offsprings,
in this, the first town I had ever seen. Half the
population were related to the Williams family.

While here the old cemetery was visited, so as
to tread on soil where my father was buried,
when I was only one year old.

A trip out to Big Hill to visit my old boyhood
friend, Christian Zipprian and his family, ended
our visit to this part of the county.

My intention was to start up the old Chisholm
cattle trail on March first, but as the time drew
near, the horse-flies and mosquitos became so bad,
causing my two pet horses so much misery, that
I gave up the trip. These horses had been raised
by me in Santa Fe, New Mexico, where there are
no such insects to torment the life out of a horse.

The trip up the old trail would have been during
the worst fly and mosquito time. Hence I concluded to avoid this by sometime, in the future, starting down the trail form Abilene, Kansas, early in
the fall, reaching the Gulf coast during the winter
season.

About the first of March, in Bay City, my
horses and outfit were put into a box-car, on the

THE AUTHOR.

A. T. & S. F. Ry. and started back to their home in New Mexico's capital city.

Of course Eat 'Em Up Jake had a nice bed in the same car with the horses. He was leaving this coast country with the satisfaction of knowing that he had taught the dog population to respect his high breeding. In every town visited he had to fight his way to respect. Often half a dozen dogs would jump onto him at the same time. No matter how many, it ended the same with Jake as victor. He never would pick a fight himself, but was always there when it ended.

The dogs were like the people, they had never seen a Russian wolf-hound before, I could have sold hundreds of Jake's pups had they been in existence. The six, which were on my ranch at Santa Fe, were snapped up quick when we first landed in Bay City. I wrote the man in charge of my place, Mr. Geo. S. Tweedy, to ship them down by express, which he did.

Poor Eat 'Em Up Jake, about a year after returning home, dropped over dead while Mrs. H. M. Martin was patting him on the head. He received a decent burial by Geo. S. Tweedy.

More than fifty of his pups had been sold, and given to friends.

Eat 'Em Up Jake, Jr., one of Jake's pups can be seen any day, at the present writing, on the streets of Santa Fe, following his kind master, Mr. "Jack" F. Collins. He doesn't think any of the fine Navajo blankets in his curio store is any too good for this high bred dog, (for whom he has refused a cash $500 offer) to stretch himself out on while napping.

It seems that these Russian wolf hounds enjoy sleeping on valuable rugs. While on our trip in southern Texas, Eat 'Em Up Jake had several fine parlor doors thrown wide open, so that he could stretch out on valuable rugs, the kind women folks thinking he made a fine picture while thus taking a restful dog nap.

At one of these swell homes in Palacios, Texas, owned by Mr. and Mrs. John T. Price, Jake was in the habit of slipping away from me, so as to stretch himself on a fine brussels carpet. Even if his feet were muddy, good Mrs. Price would throw the door open when he stood on his hind feet and rapped for admittance.

Eat 'Em Up Jake came by his name honestly. While on the Laramie plains in Wyoming, as a supposed outlaw, I traded a watch for this half starved, lanky Russian wolf hound. I also traded my gentle saddle pony for a wild broncho.

On leaving the Jim Kirkbright ranch I had a forty mile ride to make over a wild stretch of country.

The day was very warm, and when about ten miles on our journey the pup gave out completely. There was nothing to do but shoot him or put him on my broncho. The latter course was adopted.

Riding up by the side of the panting pup I leaned over and grabbed him by the neck. When I started to rise up with the wooly bundle of bones the bucking contest began. The pup was thrown in front of me. Every time the broncho struck the ground my whole weight was thrown onto the pup's empty bread basket. For about five minutes the air was full of yelping.

About noon we reached a lake and I stopped to eat lunch. I shot a mud-hen in the lake and was skinning it for the pup. He smelled the blood and made a grab for the bird. He ate everything, feathers, bill and legs, and right there got his name of Eat 'Em Up Jake.

I had to come back to New Mexico to learn the true story of how the old Chisholm cattle trail derived its name.

This information was secured from Mr. David M. Sutherland, a highly respected citizen of Alamogordo, a nice little city which sprang into existence near old Victoria's rendezvous, Dog Canyon.

I had known Mr. Sutherland by reputation for over thirty years, hence I could rely on this information being truthful. He didn't have to depend altogether on memory, as he had kept a diary of the cattle drive in 1871.

Here follows the true story of the Chisholm Trail as told to me by Mr. Sutherland, and con-

firmed through corresponding with old-timers in
Wichita, Kansas:

In about the year 1867 the United States Government concluded to move the more than 3,000
Wichita and affiliated tribes of Indians, known
as the Caddos, Wacos, Andarkos, etc., to a new
reservation in the southern part of the Indian Territory.

Their camp was located on the Arkansas River
near where Chisholm and Cow-Skin creeks empty
into that stream. They had been moved there by
the government during the Rebellion. Major Henry Shanklin was in charge of them.

Previous to the time of moving these Indians
to their new reservation Major Shanklin made a
deal with a rich half-breed "Squaw-man" by the

JESSE CHISHOLM,
Father of the Chisholm Trail.

name of Jesse Chisholm, to open a trail, and es-
tablish supply depots through the Indian Terri-

tory to Red River, the dividing line of Texas and
the "Nation."

With a large train of ox-teams Jesse Chisholm
went to Ft. Leavenworth on the Missouri River, to
load up with Government supplies.

On his reutrn to the camp,   on the Arkansas
River, 100 wild ponies were bought for the trip
through the Indian Territory.

These were used to settle the quick-sand in the
treacherous streams of Salt Fork the Cimarron,
the North Canadian and the South Canadian.

Ahead of the heavily loaded wagons this band
of ponies were driven back and forth, many times,
to settle the quick-sand.

Dug-outs were built at certain points, and a supply of grub, etc., left, for the Indians and Soldiers, to follow later.

The more than 3000 Indians with their thousands of ponies, along with the many mounted Soldiers, traveling in the ruts made by Jesse Chisholm's heavily loaded wagons made a plain road-
way. It was christened the Chisholm trail, and
over its surface passed millions of long-horn cattle in the years following.

After the Indians had vacated their camp the
Government sold the land, and the present city of
Wichita, Kansas, was established on the old camp
ground.

When the Atchison, Topeka, and Santa Fe Railroad reached the town of Wichita, and built ship-

ping pens, a few years later, the enterprising citizens began planning to turn the trail herds away from Baxter Springs, in the south-east corner of Kansas, into Wichita.

In the closing years of the '60's, the Union Pacific Railroad had reached Abilene, Kansas, further north, and that town backed by the Union Pacific railroad company, laid plans to get some of the Texas cattle trade.

In the spring of 1870 Mr. David M. Sutherland, who was associated with Major Henry Shanklin, went to Bosque County, Texas, and purchased a herd of long-horn cattle, which were driven over the new Chisholm trail to Wichita, thence to Abilene.

The following spring, 1871, Major Shanklin and Mr. Sutherland were employed by the Union Pacific Railway Company to turn the cattle drive away from Baxter Springs, onto the Chisholm trail, through the Indian Territory.

Mr. Sutherland went to Gainesville, Texas, to meet the Baxter Springs trail herds and induce the owners and bosses to turn west to Red River station, where they would strike the Chisholm trail and have good grass and water all the way through the Indian Territory.

During the season Mr. Sutherland, and the boosters sent by the town of Wichita, succeeded in turning most of the herds to the Chisholm trail.

Mr. Sutherland says that in April, 1871 he made a cut-off trail with plows, from Pilot Point to Boliver, in the state of Texas, for the herds to follow. That from Boliver to Red River Station there was already a plain wagon road.

It is said that the Wichita boosters paid as high as $500 to owners and bosses to induce them to change their course from Baxter Springs to the Chisholm trail at Red River Station.

During the next season, 1872, the whole trail drive continued north from Austin, Texas, to Red River Station, and the entire route to Abiline, Kansas, became known as the Chisholm trail.

At the Montopolis crossing on the Colorado River, two and a half miles below the Capital City of Austin, Texas, the many small trails from all over the Gulf Coast merged into the Chisholm trail, which was now a solid road-way, several hundred yards wide, all the way to Wichita and Abilene, Kansas.

Every season for ten long years this old trail was used. At least 5,000,000 head of cattle, and a half million Spanish mares, with which to stock new horse ranches on the northern ranges, were driven over it during those years.

Some individual owners drove many herds each season.

I can only recall the names of a few of the most prominent trail drovers. A Mr. Fant, of Golliad, Texas, King and Kennedy, of Corpus Christi, Un-

cle Henry Stevens and the firm of Millett and Ma-
berry, I believe drove the greatest number of
herds each season.

As large trail drivers, Hood and Hughes, W. B.
Grimes, "Shanghai" Pierce, Capt. George Littlefield, Charlie and Tom Word, the Lovings,
Driscols, Slaughters, Collins' and Pryors were
prominent names on the trail. At the present writing Col. Ike Pryor is president of the Texas Cattlemen's Association, with headquarters in San
Antonio, Texas.

The Days, Dan Waggoner and Hunter and Evans were well known on the Chisholm trail.

No doubt King and Kennedy would take the
premium as the largest trail drivers.

This Mr. King, who, with his partner, Mr. Kennedy, owned the largest cattle ranch in Texas, was
the cause of the word "Cattle-King," as applied
to large cattle owners, being incorporated into our
language. It started thus:

In the early days when speaking of a Mr. King
the question would be asked: "Which King do you
mean?" The answer would be: "The Cattle
King"—meaning Mr. King of the firm of King
and Kennedy. He was "The Cattle King" in name
as well as a Cattle King in the ownership of the
largest cattle ranch in Texas.

Dan Waggoner was one of the great "Cattle
Kings" of Texas. He got his start in the early
'70s by buying new Mitchell wagons on the Mis-

souri river, and with oxen and mules, hauling them, trailed together, down the Chisholm trail into Texas. These wagons being traded for wild long-horn steers, which were then cheap and a drug on the market, while the wagons were scarce and commanded a high price.

"Uncle" Steve Birchfield, now a wealthy resident of El Paso, Texas, with ranches along the Mexico border, was also a prominent trail driver. I first met him in Wichita, Kansas, in 1876, and in the fall of 1915, about thirty-seven years later, I spent more than a week with him at the Park Hotel in Las Cruces, New Mexico. Of course we "harked back" to the good old days of long-horn cattle.

One of the stories he related will show the nature of some of those who drove "up the Chisholm trail" to Kansas.

In 1873 "Uncle" Steve Birchfield made up a herd of steers in Uvalde County, Texas.

At the same time a man known as "Black Bob" had a herd ready to start "up the trail." Owing to the danger of Indians, in passing through the Indian "Nation," Birchfield and "Black Bob" agreed to keep their herds close together.

On their arrival at Red River, "Black Bob" had a bad stampede during a stormy night and lost a few steers, by them mixing up with local range cattle.

The next day both herds were put across Red River into the "Nation."

Now "Black Bob" sent most of his crew back into Texas to gather up the lost steers. He told his men to gather all steers with muddy feet, showing that they had been running in mud during the stampede.

When the crew returned they had about 700 head of muddy footed steers, owned by various northern Texas cattlemen. These were put into "Black Bob's" herd and the journey continued.

In order to avoid the state inspector at Red River station, the boys had crossed the river in the night, below the trail crossing.

Now "Black Bob" had a large size herd. He had no mess-wagon, the grub and bedding being carried on pack ponies.

On reaching Pond Creek, near the Kansas border, "Black Bob" came very near starting a war with a large band of Osage Indians, who were headed west on a big buffalo hunt.

Arriving near the town of Wichita, their camps were pitched close together. Then part of each crew went to Wichita to celebrate.

"Uncle" Steve Birchfield says he secured a room in the new Occidental Hotel, which was not yet completed. His room fronted on the main street, and it had no window sashes in the place left open for a window.

Being tired he went to bed early. About daylight he heard pistol shots and yelling on the street. He went to the open window and looked out. There he saw some of "Black Bob's" drunken cowboys charging up and down the street on their ponies.

There were two gun stores in town, each having a large wooden gun for a sign. Two of "Black Bob's" cowboys tore loose these wooden guns and were carrying them across the front of their saddles.

Soon a crowd of "fool hoe-men" who had come to town the evening previous to buy supplies, and who were up early, so as to get an early start for home, collected in front of the Occidental Hotel. The boys with the wooden guns charged up to the crowd and asked if they had heard of the Osage Indians turning out on the war-path. They told of being in a battle with the Indians the day before at Pond Creek, in the "Nation," and of how they had ridden all night to reach Wichita.

They said the Indians had killed many white men, and were now headed for Medicine Lodge, one hundred miles west of Wichita.

"Uncle" Steve says many of these "fool hoemen" didn't wait long enough to hear the whole news of the great Indian outbreak. They ran in every direction to get their teams to hurry home and protect their families.

The news spread like wild-fire, and soon reached the Governor of the state, in Topeka. He at

once called out the state militia, and hurried them
to Medicine Lodge.

There being no funds to pay these militia men,
he sent an agent to Medicine Lodge to organize a
new county, so as to vote bonds to pay the militia. .

The new county of Barbour was organized, with
Medicine Lodge as the county seat.

There not being sufficient voters in the new
county, the soldier boys were allowed to cast a
vote, so as to issue $60,000 worth of county bonds,
to pay the soldiers.

An agent was sent East to sell these bonds, and
he skipped out with the cash received for them.

The militia finally had a skirmish and rounded
up the band of friendly Osage Indians, whose
anger had been stirred up by "Black Bob" at
Pond Creek. Thus did Barbour County, Kansas,
get a place on the state map.

These "fool hoe-men" as we "locoed" cowboys
called the new settlers, had a good reason for
their excitement, as, a few years previous,
the Osage Indians had turned out on the warpath
and murdered many white men in the southern
part of Kansas, their reservation being over the
line in the "Nation".

CHAPTER XI.

A BLOOD SPATTERED ROAD IN NEW MEXICO.

I SERVE TWO YEARS AS NEW MEXICO RANGER.

In the fall of 1915 I spent several weeks at Tularosa on that blood spattered road between Lincoln and Las Cruces. While here I saw the fresh blood still in the road where the last man was killed, a short time previous.

This life-blood had flown from the veins of Ralph Connell, a lawyer and stockman of Tularosa. He was driving a bunch of cattle up to the Mescalaro Indian Reservation, where he had a contract to furnish beef to the Indians.

With him were his twelve year old daughter, and two Mexican cowboys. When about two miles out of Tularosa, in front of Jim Porter's nice residence, a bullet from a high-power rifle pierced his heart, and he fell from his horse. He and cowboy Jim Porter were bitter enemies, and the supposition is that Porter sent the bullet on its deadly mission.

In Tularosa lived my cowboy friend, John P. Meadows, one of the most law abiding men of the age. Whenever a murder was committed he was in the saddle, on the side of Justice. He had been one of sheriff Pat Garrett's most trusted deputies and friends, until that fearless peace-officer met death, on this same blood-spattered road. He was on his way to Las Cruces when shot and killed.

My friend Capt. Fred Fornoff, then at the head of the New Mexico Mounted Police, who investigated the matter, feels confident that desperado Jim Miller fired the bullet that killed Pat Garrett, although another man got the credit for it, as, according to Capt. Fornoff's statement, it was a put up job.

But this "bad" man Miller, who had been a killer of men in Texas for years, met his just dues by being swung up to a tree shortly afterwards.

He had just gone back to his old stamping ground in Oklahoma and was hanged by a mob.

A friend of mine, who lived in the neighborhood, told me the facts in the case.

The mob were after Miller and his chum, who camped in an old barn that night. A stranger had come along and camped with them, not knowing who they were.

When the mob stormed the barn the stranger was hanged with the other two, as he had been caught in bad company. But, when too late, it was found out that he had accidentally struck up with these two "bad" men.

John P. Meadows was born and raised within fifteen miles of Pat Garrett, in Lee County, Alabama, the date of his birth being May 26th, 1854, and his birth-place being the town of Mechanicsville. He drifted to Eastland County, Texas, in 1873.

JOHN P. MEADOWS.

In the fall of 1874 he hired out to George Knox to kill buffalo for their hides. Here he met Pat Garrett, who had just killed his first man, a Mr. Glen.

The following year John Meadows worked for Johnny Larn and John Sillman—"two of the meanest men who ever lived," as Meadows expressed it.

This is the same Johnny Larn who was shot to death in jail by a mob, and the same John Sillman who, I am sure, killed the two Mexican boys and stole their band of sheep, in 1878.

Up to 1877, John Meadows was a buffalo hunter, He then became a cowboy for the Millett brothers, who owned a large cattle ranch, and drove many herds "up the Chisholm trail."

In 1879 Meadows and my old cowboy friend, Tom Harris, drifted to Ft. Sumner, New Mexico, where they met "Billy the Kid," who befriended them, which touched a soft spot in John Meadow's heart. Since then Meadows has been an honored citizen of New Mexico.

The above mentioned Tom Harris was the leader in the first and only cowboy strike which ever took place. This unique strike for higher wages was pulled off in the Panhandle of Texas, about the year 1886. The Panhandle cattlemen hired Pat Garrett and a crowd of fighting rangers to put down the trouble. Some blood was spilled and many enemies made while the strike lasted. Tascosa was the striker's headquarters.

Ever since the spring of 1882, when I bade Mr. and Mrs. George Nesbeth goodby in Las Cruces, and they expressed a fear that Pat Cohglin would have them murdered, I have had a desire to see their graves, and to learn the truth of their murder. Therefore, during my stay in Tularosa, this desire was gratified.

John P. Meadows had helped to run down the murderers, and to lay the bodies of Mr. and Mrs. Nesbeth, their adopted daughter, and the stranger traveling with them, in their graves. He gave me the full details of the case, the substance of which follows:

With a covered wagon, drawn by two horses, they left Las Cruces for their new home at Blaziers Mill. They were all murdered at the point of the White Sands, about half way between Las Cruces and Tularosa, on August 17th, 1882. They were killed by two Mexicans at night, while in camp.

A prospector hunting lost burros found their swollen bodies quite a while afterwards.

The horses and everything of value, except the wagon and harness, had been taken away by the murderers, and this led to their identification, later.

When run down the murderers proved to be Rupert Lara and Maximo Appodaco. In their con-

fession at the trial they swore that Pat Cohglin
had hired them, for $1000, to kill Mr. and Mrs.
Nesbeth. That they had to kill the little girl and
the stranger to prevent them giving the alarm.

Both were convicted for the crime. Shortly afterwards Appodaco committed suicide, and Lara
was hanged by the neck until dead.

Pat Cohglin was never brought to trial. His
money, no doubt, saved his neck, as he was an expert at using his wealth where it would do the
most good for himself, and for the wife he swapped for. When he left Texas he swapped wives
with his brother-in-law, they being married to sis-
ters.

This information I received from Captain F. B.
Taylor, of the United States Army. His letter
was written in Ft. Leavenworth Kans., and dated
Feb. 4th, 1886. Here is a quotation from this personal letter to me:

"That little stone Jacal where the "Kid" was
captured gave me shelter once from a blinding
sand storm. In those days it was occupied by Mexicans.

"Pat Cohglin was well known to all my regi-
ment before he moved from Texas to Tularosa.
He made a queer trade, or swap, when he and his
brother-in-law, Taylor, swapped wives at the time
they broke partnership. A brief history of how he
acquired possession of that store, on the plaza in
Tularosa, would make interesting reading. I was

stationed at Ft. Stanton, New Mexico, for several years.''

My old friend ''Buck'' Prude, who owned the trading store at the Mescalero Indian Reservation, took John Meadows and me in an automobile to the Indian Reservation.

On the way there we stopped at a Mexican's house to see the bullet marks in the door, as a reminder of one battle which took place on this blood-spattered road.

In this battle two of John Goodes cowboys, Johnson and ''Dutch,'' murdered Howe, the owner of this ranch, this being in the spring of 1887.

With the help of Indian trailers John P. Meadows ran down these two murderers, and assisted in their conviction.

At Blaziers Mill, within two miles of the Indian Agency, we visited the grave-yard on a round mound, where rest the bodies of poor Mr. and Mrs. George Nesbeth, as also those of the little girl and the stranger who were murdered with them.

As Meadows helped to bury them he could point out each grave. He also pointed out the graves of the men killed in the battle here between ''Billy the Kid's'' gang, and the Seven River warriors. In this bloody battle my friend George Coe, now a respected ranchman of Glencoe, New Mexico, lost one of his fingers. His brother, Frank Coe, a well-to-do ranchman on the Riodoso river, was also in this battle, helping "Billy the Kid."

After the Lincoln County war the Coe brothers, being law abiding men, quit the "Kid's" gang.

I spent two days in the Mescalaro Indian Agency as the guest of the Indian Agent, Mr. Jefferies, and his lovely wife.

Strange to relate, here I found Mr. Miller, in charge of the Indian Police, holding down the same job that he held when I first met him in the spring of 1881, at which time Maj. W. H. Llewellyn, of rough rider fame, was the Agent. Thirty-three years is a long time to hang onto one job.

On returning to Santa Fe from this trip I made preparations to start for Abilene, Kansas, mounted on Rowdy, with Pat as a pack-horse, to ride down the Old Chisholm cattle trail to the Gulf Coast of Texas, to mark the prominent places for the benefit of posterity, and to satisfy a foolish desire.

As markers I aimed to use a large pair of aluminum steer horns, with the name "Chisholm Trail." on each horn. They were to be fastened onto two inch galvanized pipe, set into a cement foundation.

I had made a deal with an Erie, Pa. firm to furnish these horns at $2.80 a pair, I figured that each marker, complete, would cost $20.

In some way the Wichita, Kansas, Daily Beacon

heard of my plans and intentions, and came out with a column and a half write-up. Other papers copied the article.

Shortly after, I received a letter from my old-time friend, Chas. H. Moore, Vice President of the National City Bank, in Kansas City, Mo., with instructions to draw on him for the cost of one marker, to be placed on the old trail where it crossed Bluff Creek, on the line of Kansas and Oklahoma, about two miles south of Caldwell.

This is as far as the Chisholm trail came to being marked, as the late war with Germany caused aluminum metal to soar skyward in price, so that the Erie, Pa. firm cancelled their agreement with me. Hence my trip was given up—and the old trail may never be marked.

Early in the spring of 1916 my friend, Governor Wm. C. McDonald, persuaded me to accept a position as Ranger, with a commission as Mounted Police, for the Cattle Sanitary Board of New Mexico.

Therefore, on the first day of March I started south, mounted on Rowdy, with the pack on Pat, and Jumbo, an offspring of Eat 'Em Up Jake, chasing jack rabbits on ahead.

Governor McDonald had selected Carrizozo, the present county seat of Lincoln County, as my headquarters.

Bill Owens, a fighting son-of-a-gun, was selected as my partner, we to have jurisdiction over

seven counties, north of the Old Mexico border, to
run down outlaws and stock thieves.

But poor Bill Owens only lasted a short time. In
a fight with two Mexican cattle thieves, at Abo
Pass, he was shot through the lungs and lay at the
point of death for a long time. This ended his use-
fulness as a mounted Ranger.

After he had fallen, Bill Owens emptied his pistol into the thief who had shot him. Both of the
thieves were killed.

Near the edge of Carrizozo Governor McDonald
had his fine ranch home, at Carrizozo Springs,
and here we met often to discuss my work, much
of which was done on the large Block cattle range,
owned by McDonald and his associates, along the
northern foot-hills of the Capitan mountains.

On several occasions Governor McDonald's
ranch manager, Mr. Truman A. Spencer, who was
married to the Governor's only daughter, took me
on hurried trips in his fine large automobile. Mr.
Spencer is ''shore'' some driver, when it comes
to swiftness, and carefulness.

When in Carrizozo I made Dr. M. G. Paden's
drug-store and hospital my loafing place. The
doctor was one of the young ''bucks'' batching
with W. C. McDonald, Jim Brent, and Andy Rob-
enson, near my camp in White Oaks during the
winter of 1880-81. Later he went to Louisville,
Kentucky, and studied medicine, which made him
one of New Mexico's leading physicians.

In Carrizozo my old friend, Mr. George Ulrick, President of the Exchange Bank, who lived in White Oaks during the boom days there, took me up to his fine new home and introduced me to his good wife. He showed me one of the nicest furnished rooms in the house, and said this should be mine so long as my headquarters were in Carrizozo, free of rent.

Of course I had to decline the kind offer, as it would be taking advantage of good nature. I had already rented a nice room in the home of Charlie Ross, who was connected with Dr. Paden's drug store. This remained my home for over two years, during my visits to the town. Mrs. Ross and their young son, Charlie, made my life pleasant.

Some of my work was done around White Oaks, and I was compelled to drag into Court, for cattle stealing, men whom I knew when they were boys. It was a matter of business with me, still they will never live long enough to forgive me.

In White Oaks I was treated royally by old time friends, among them being Judge John Y. Hewett and Charlie D. Mayer, the leading merchant there. Mayer had married Ina Wauchope, grand-daughter of the old placer miner, John Wilson, who helped put White Oaks on the map. I knew her when she was a pretty young miss, thinking of the happy day when she would become a woman. She still hangs on to some of her good looks and all of her winning ways.

I found Arabella and the Palos Springs, Mexican settlements, at the east end of the Capitan mountains, to be a nest of cattle thieves, although many law abiding men lived there.

Governor McDonald had told me that these Mexican thieves would try to run me out of the country, as they had done with other officers sent in there to catch them stealing Block cattle.

My work in Arabella proved exciting, and showed the ignorance and viciousness of the Mexican Justice of the Peace there, who protected the cattle thieves.

I made the mistake of trying the first four thieves arrested by me in the Justice of the Peace Court. The "Judge" put the thieves on the witness stand to hear their side of the story, but wouldn't allow me to put my witness' on the stand.

The father of one of the thieves, who in the early days was mixed up in one of the coldest blooded murders ever pulled off, acted as lawyer for the defence. He ruled the Court.

When it was over the Court freed the prisoners and assessed the cost of the case, $25, against me, giving orders to the armed constable to not allow me to leave the court room until the costs were paid.

With my hand on my pistol I started for the door. The constable with his hand on his pistol started to stop me. I told him to stand back, which he did, thus preventing the floor from being smeared with blood.

In front of the court room which was full of Mexicans, "Red" Dale, one of the Block cowboys, sat on his horse holding my mount by the bridle reins.

Keeping my eyes on the crowd, which had followed me out of the door, my mount was reached. Then pulling the high power rifle from the scabbard on the saddle, I rode away with it in my hand, ready for action.

After galloping two miles west I allowed "Red" Dale to continue on the wagon road back to the Block round-up camp, in charge of Mr. Lloyd Taylor.

I then cut across the mountains for the Arroyo Seco ranch, owned by Governor McDonald, a distance of nine miles.

Arriving there Mrs. Roberts got me a quick meal. Then I rounded up nine head of stolen horses, in a small pasture, and started with them for the Block ranch, twenty miles west.

A couple of days previous I had captured the band of horses from outlaw "Chon" Romero and his son. This "Chon" Romero was a daring outlaw. Soon after, he was shot dead on the street of Arabella by one of Sheriff Walker Hyde's Mexican deputies.

Cowboy Johnny Roberts, assisted me in getting the band of horses started on the road.

I was barely out of sight when the Arabella constable and a deputy, both armed with high power rifles, and having a warrant for my arrest, rode up to the Arroyo Seco ranch house. They asked for me, and Mr. Roberts, who had just returned, told them that I had left in an automobile for Carrizozo. An auto had been there a short time previous, and the fresh tracks showed in the road. Now the disappointed officers, who had followed my tracks, after the Justice of the Peace had issued a warrant for my arrest, returned home.

I reached the Block ranch just in time to get a swift automobile night ride with Mr. Truman Spencer.

The next morning in Carrizozo I had a talk with District Attorney H. B. Hamilton, and from him found out that it would have been a case of murder had I killed the constables while they held a warrant for my arrest. I was under the impression that these officers had no lawful right to arrest me outside of their precinct—hence I had made up my mind to fight them to a finis,h had they overtaken me. It was lucky for me that Mr. Roberts turned them back.

Now I swore out warrants before a Justice of the Peace in Carrizozo for the four prisoners whom the Arabella "Judge" had set free. Then Deputy Sheriff John B. Baird—whose father was a fearless Texas sheriff, whom I knew—and I drove to Arabella, a distance of seventy-five miles, and arrested the four released prisoners.

At their trial in Carrizozo they were put under a bond of $1000 each to appear at the next term of the District Court in Carrizozo.

Much of my future work was done around Arabella, and the thieving gang became docile. I received much valuable assistance from cowboy Henry Rogers, who had charge of the Block ranch at Steel Springs. Also that prince of a good fellow, Phil Blanchard, whom I knew when he was a boy in White Oaks, and who now owns a large stock ranch, gave me much assistance, at the risk of making bitter enemies in Arabella, near where his ranch was situated.

Many old wells in the Arabella neighborhood were full of Block cattle hides thrown in after the animals were butchered. From one well seventy-five hides were taken out.

Near the town of Encinoso we had a laughable experience with Mexican cattle thieves. Cowboys Johnny Littleton, a Mr. Stratton and I made a raid on a settlement, searching several houses for fresh beef. At the Baca home the folks willingly showed me through the house, and pointed out some goat meat cooking.

When I stepped around the outside of the house I saw Jumbo eying a large box. It proved to be full of fresh beef.

At the Lucero home the table was set for dinner.

The family swore they had no beef of any kind. I opened the oven door and brought forth the head of a yearling baked to a nice brown. It seemed a shame to rob these people of their dinner, but I needed the head as evidence.

In a cabin on the premises we found the whole beef. It had been butchered inside the cabin and the door kept locked. In the ashes in the fireplace I dug out the horns of the animal, and the piece of hide containing the Block brand.

Before hauling this nice fat beef away to be distributed among our friends I gave the Lucero family part of a hind quarter to pay for the head taken out of the oven, so that the two pretty young daughters would not be deprived of their dinner.

The father and son, and young Baca were arrested and taken to Carrizozo, where they were put under bond to appear before Judge Medler in the District Court.

They employed my friend Col. Geo. W. Prichard to defend them, which meant the wearing out of their cases in the courts.

After war broke out with Germany, Col. Prichard secured Baca's freedom; so that he could join the army.

In order to gather up stray horses I attended a spring horse round-up on the Mescalaro Indian Reservation, putting in about two weeks there. The round-up crews were all Indians, and the way they abused horses made my heart bleed. They have no more mercy for a wild broncho than for a rattle snake. And they don't know the first principle of handling wild horses.

Some of my work was done on the Riodoso River, in the Glencoe neighborhood, and there I enjoyed life. It seemed like going back to my early cowboy life, where everyone seemed like a father, mother, brother or sister.

I generally put up at Bert Bonnells fine home. He was a son of Mr. Ed Bonnell who ran the lumber yard in White Oaks in the early days, and whom I held in high esteem.

Bert had married one of Frank Coe's pretty daughters, and she is "shore" a peach as a singer, musician, and knowing how to make visitors feel at home.

Here I attended many dances which generally wound up in a regular old fashioned Texas "hodown."

Below the Bonnell ranch Mr. Frank Coe has his fine home, and his whole family are musicians. And one mile above lives Mr. George Coe and his fine family. These Coe brothers were in many battles with "Billy the Kid" during the bloody Lincoln County war. George Coe takes pride in the loss of one finger in the battle at Blaziers Mill.

It was near George Coe's ranch where Mr. Tunstall was killed by the Seven River warriors, which started the Lincoln County war.

Being a Justice of the Peace, I brought some of

my cattle stealing cases into Mr. Coe's Court. In arresting Mexican thieves on the Riodoso, I was assisted by Will Coe and Lon Hunter, two fearless cowboys. My old friend, Mr. J. V. Tully, the postmaster and merchant in Glencoe, who also owns a large cattle ranch, assisted me in many ways.

The Mexicans are not all thieves by any means. As a rule they are a law abiding people, and in some ways have got the "Americans" beat a mile. They are the most hospitable race on earth. Money don't count when it comes to caring for a tired and hungry stranger. They will give up their bed and sleep on the floor, themselves, to make it pleasant for a "Gringo," as the "Americans" are called.

No matter how poor a Mexican family is, you will find the inside of their house neat and clean. The worst fault of the woman-folks is their fondness for babies and fice dogs. The smaller the baby or puppy the greater the affection.

While attending one term of court in Carrizozo I was taught how old "Father Time" heals wounds. I was introduced to Mr. Augustin Kayser, who owns a small cattle ranch near Corona. He remembered my name, and asked: "Say, in 1872, when you were a boy, did someone steal your rain blanket, one stormy night?"

Of course I remembered it, as, for several years

it had left a bitter feeling in my heart, against the thief.

He then continued: "Well, Charlie, I am the thief who kept dry that night under your blanket. Of course I felt sorry for you, but it was a case of self protection, as I had lost my slicker," (rain coat.).

We were putting up a herd of long-horn steers for the trail, I, being on the last guard, had gone to bed, leaving my saddled night horse tied to a tree near by. On my saddle was a Mexican rain blanket, used instead of a slicker. They are made narrow and long, with a slit in the center to stick your head into, the fringed ends coming down below the boot tops. On getting wet they become hard, and turn water like rubber.

On this particular night a severe rain storm sprang up and every sleeping cowboy had to spring onto his night-horse.

A stampede followed, and during the balance of the night I suffered greatly from the cold spring rain. The next morning my blanket was found lying on my bed, the rain having ceased.

In southern Texas these fancy colored blankets were plentiful, but I never saw but one of them in the Panhandle country. During a cold blizzard, or rain storm there, if you happened to see a Mexican blanket coming towards you, or going in an opposite direction, you could bet your last dollar that Jim East's head, covered with a gold and silver mounted sombrero, was sticking out of the slit in the center.

During my two years work as Ranger and Mounted Police I had the pleasure of visiting some of my old stamping grounds, such as Rosswell, Capitan, Nogal, Ft. Stanton and Lincoln.

Capitan can boast of the biggest high-school building, and the biggest general mercantile establishment, owned by two wide-awake cattlemen, George and Will Titsworth, in Lincoln County. Also the biggest little weekly newspaper, "The Mountaineer," owned and conducted by a big man with a big heart and a bigger name, Mr. Neil H. Bigger. As Mr. Bigger has passed the spring chicken age he couldn't get out such a spicy local paper without the help of his broad-gauge son. Mr. Sam. J. Bigger.

Capitan also has at her back door one of the largest cattle ranches, the Block outfit, in the whole state of New Mexico. Cowboy Frank Ellis, and Jim Woodland are permanent fixtures on this well conducted ranch, and they are both beginning to turn grey over worrying about the welfare of these thousands of fine white-face cattle.

As a boy Jim Woodland drifted from Texas with Tom O'Phalliard, "Billy the Kid's" dearest chum. Instead of turning outlaw he became a deputy sheriff under sheriff Kimbrall, which position he held when I first met him at White Oaks, in 1880.

In Lincoln the old two story Court-house, where
"Billy the Kid" pulled off his great and daring
stunt, still stands as a monument to remind old-
timers of the days when Lincoln County covered
a territory nearly 200 miles square. Since then
she has been cut up into several counties. In Roswell and along the Pecos river the greatest change
has taken place. In this lovely little city of Roswell
where, in 1881 Tom Emory grazed the LX steers
on the grassy flat in front of Capt. J. C. Lea's
store, while we were attending the round-ups on
John Chisum's range, now stands costly business
blocks.

And five miles south, where we attended hodown dances in the Texas settlement called Pumpkin Row, there are now fine homes and orchards.

In fact the whole Pecos valley clear down to the
Texas line is a garden spot, with little cities and
towns by the score, Artesia, Carlsbad, Dexter,
Dayton, Lake Arthur, Malaga, Hagerman, Lake-
wood and Hope being the leading embryo cities.

In 1881 this was all Government land, only fit
for grazing. A few years later Chas. B. Eddy,
now living on easy street in the city of New York,
woke up to the fact that it would make a farming
country. He and his brother John owned a large
cattle ranch at Salida, Colorado.

In the spring of 1882 the Eddy brothers moved
some of their cattle from Colorado and establish-

ed a cattle ranch near where Carlsbad, the county seat of Eddy County, is now located.

In the early winter of 1882, while riding down the Pecos River, I passed the new adobe ranch house of the Eddy brothers, only a few hundred yards east of the road.

A man sitting on the west side of the building waved at me. I rode over and Mr. C. B. Eddy introduced himself to me and wanted to know if there was any news of importance up at Roswell.

He was alone, as his cowboys had gone out on the range to look after the cattle. It being at the noon hour he cooked a nice meal for me and himself.

Five years later, in 1887, while doing detective work I boarded a stage coach in Carthage, on the Rio Grande river, for a ninety mile ride to White Oaks.

The only passengers in the stage coach, besides myself, were a lady and a fine looking, dark complected gentleman of middle age.

This gentleman kept eying me, but I pretended not to notice it.

When about half way on our journey he spoke to me, saying: "Say, partner, didn't you ride down the Pecos River in 1882, mounted on a white crop-eared horse?"

Of course I answered "yes," then he continued: "My name is Charles B. Eddy, and I cooked dinner for you at my ranch."

Now we shook hands and "harked back" to the cattle days.

In White Oaks we put up at the Ozane Hotel, and here Mr. Eddy gave me a confidential tip. He advised me to throw up any other business that I might be engaged in and hurry to the Pecos Valley and secure some land. He said he was now on the way to Roswell, and that within a year the whole Pecos Valley would be on a boom, as he had succeeded in getting millions of dollars with which to develop that country, in the way of new railroads and irrigation dams. But I didn't have sense enough to take his advice.

In 1888 the valley was on a big boom, and the Government land was being gobbled up fast. In many ways it was being stolen from the Government. A friend of mine spent the summer there doing detective work for the Pinkertons. He told me of a case where a certain individual, representing a large irrigation Co., went to El Paso and hired sixty old Mexico Mexicans at one dollar a day each, with free grub, to take up Pecos Valley land.

Of course these Mexicans had to swear that they were citizens of the United States, in order to take up land. They entered one whole section of land each, in the choicest spots, under the desert land laws.

When the water from the large new reservoir was turned onto the land, and a patent secured, these sixty Mexicans deeded the property to the Company.

Now the "foxy" individual, for whom my friend was doing the detective work, had these sixty citizens of Old Mexico change their names and go further up the river, towards Roswell, and enter sixty more sections under the desert law.

This land, with a water right, was worth $100 an acre, so you can imagine the value of these 120 sections, a total of 438,000 acres, secured through fraud. It virtually put millions of dollars into the company's hands when the land was sold to farmers. Still it did good by developing the country quickly.

On my way back to Santa Fe, after finishing the work as Ranger for the Cattle Sanitary Board, they being out of funds to pay the twelve Rangers scattered throughout the state, I had the experience of looking into the barrel of a big Colts pistol, while a drunken man's trembling finger was resting on the trigger. I had to endure the agony for about a minute, until the drunken Arkansawyer made his little speech against officers of the law.

This stunt was pulled off in a livery stable, in the town of Moriarity, by Hamp Wallace, who had got the drop on me while my pistol was lying on a bunk out of reach.

I felt sorry for poor, ignorant Hamp Wallace next day, when with tears in his eyes and voice

he plead guilty before a Justice of the Peace, in
Estancia. He was let off with a fine of $25 and
costs, and soon after departed for Arkansas where
he will feel at home while hoeing corn and cotton.

On reaching Santa Fe my cowboy outfit was
laid away, and another start made at leading the
"simple life" on my Sunny Slope Ranch near the
edge of the city. At the present writing, June 9th
1919, I am still keeping it up and dreaming of the
good old days when there were no wire fences,
or scales to weigh fresh beef on.

When the time comes for putting me under the
sod, I hope the little verse by Charles
Badger Clarke, Jr., which follows, will be
carved on my headstone. This verse was dug up
from the William E. Hawks collection of cowboy
songs as appropriate for the wind-up of a fool
cowboy's life history.

Mr. William E. Hawks, of Bennington, Vermont, a cowboy of the old school, has been fifteen
years gathering cowboy songs and data, with a
view of publishing a true history of the early day
cattle business, so that posterity will know the
class of dare-devils who paved the way for the
man with a hoe.

The hoe-man will need no history for the benefit of posterity, as he is here to stay. When once
he plants his feet on the soil, time or cyclones can-
not jar him loose:

WM. E. HAWKS

'Twas good to live when all the range
Without no fence or fuss,
Belonged in partnership with God,
The Government and us.

With skyline bounds from east to west,
With room to go and come,
I liked my fellow man the best
When he was scattered some.

When my old soul hunts range and rest
Beyond the last divide,
Just plant me on some strip of west
That's sunny, lone and wide.

Let cattle rub my headstone round,
And coyotes wail their kin,
Let hosses come and paw the mound,
But don't you fence it in.

(The End)

9 780865 345331

www.ingramcontent.com/pod-product-compliance
Lightning Source LLC
Chambersburg PA
CBHW020604270326
41927CB00005B/174